M000294914

# CONTENTS

## PREP WORK

## Harmful Ingredients

## Secret Ingredients

## Special Ingredients

## Surprise Ingredients

## Lighter Ingredients

## Frosting Your Cake

# FOREWORD

*Dr. Karen Blase*

Having earned my doctorate in Developmental and Child Psychology, I came away with five theories of child development – but had no children. Now I have five children and no theories of child development!

While I do have five children and a PhD, this statement about child development theory is, of course, not the truth with a capital "T". However, it certainly reflects the complex challenges and self-doubt that can come with parenting your teen. While those turbulent years are behind me and my grown children are a delight, I can't help but wish that I'd had Gail Manahan's book, *Is Raising Your Teen a Piece of Cake? Expert Advice for Navigating the Teen Years.* It would have been a godsend. And it would have been a very helpful resource for the many social workers, child care staff, group home parents, foster parents and educators who I have had the privilege of guiding and coaching as they worked with families and teens. Her empathy and encouragement, experience as a counselor, and her sound, practical advice would have added so much.

I have had the privilege of knowing Gail Manahan for the past 35 years. While she entered my life as my husband's niece, we quickly bonded as colleagues and friends. Through the years, I have admired her dedication, talent, success, and commitment to helping teens and families navigate the joys and trials of the teen years. Her commitment to her own professional growth and development has served her clients and her community very well, from developing renowned teen and adult self-growth seminars to decades of counseling families and teens to being honored with community awards. Now, with the publication of this parenting guide, her reach, support, and advice are available to parents, family members, and caregivers who deeply love their children but who are often frustrated, confused, frightened and concerned about creating safe passage for their teens and their family.

Gail not only offers her advice on how to approach the many types of "cakes" you encounter while parenting your teen, but she has her own winning recipe for creating this valuable guide and resource. What ingredients and recipes will you find within these pages?

First, you will find that difficult topics are made more palatable because she illustrates the many challenges through the analogy of baking different types of cakes. It's easier to approach the reality of these difficult challenges, such as drug use, mental health, eating disorders, legal issues through the cake analogies. The analogies are engaging but they never get in the way of her clarity in describing the challenges, what you can do, and offering hope for the future. You will relate to her cake recipes and are likely to find you've encountered more than one of her 'cakes' or 'special ingredients' as you raise your family.

Next, you will find healthy helpings of empathy and guilt-free guidance! Gail repeatedly stresses the importance of parents doing the best they can to use the ingredients that they have, including their parenting style, communication, love for their child and seeking professional help and support. But she also reminds us that there are many other powerful influences in a teenager's life that parents cannot control including peers, social media and messaging, relationship break-ups, friendship disappointments, and the overall angst of growing into adulthood. Her guide will help you gain perspective, understand you are not alone, and will simultaneously relieve you of guilt while turning up the temperature and telling you to avoid denial and pay attention because many teen issues can have serious consequences. A marvelously balanced recipe that will feed your soul and strengthen your parenting muscles.

Following excellent general guidance for raising your teen and using this guide, Gail engagingly takes you through 15 of the most common 'cakes' parents encounter while raising their teens. Ranging from Devil's Food Cake dealing with legal issues, to Having Your Cake and Not Eating It Too tackling eating disorders, to Upside-Down Cake, coping with divorce. You also will appreciate the just-right portions in each section. The depth of information is just-right and with enough detail to help you determine if a particular 'cake' is being baked in your family or if it is already on your plate. A quick look at the table of contents is sure to pique your interest.

Most importantly, following each challenging 'cake' recipe, you will find a section titled, *What Can I Do?* The advice is clear, practical, free of jargon, and doable for parents, family members, and caregivers of teens. And there are links and resources for you to go deeper into an area. While Gail never minimizes the risks and seriousness of the issues, she also provides honest encouragement about the future for you and your teen with a section titled, *And Here's the Good News!* Empowering and encouraging!

Parenting a teen is rewarding, worrying, challenging, stressful and frustrating. You need and deserve a knowledgeable, supportive companion on your journey. I feel confident that, Gail Manahan's parenting guide, *Is Raising Your Teen a Piece of Cake? Expert Advice for Navigating the Teen Years* is just that companion. After all, every baker needs recipes and knowledge to grow their confidence and competence – this is your guide for a guilt-free, realistic yet encouraging experience.

Karen Blase, PhD

*Karen has been a service provider, researcher, program evaluator, trainer, and published author in the human service field for over 45 years. She received her doctorate in Developmental and Child Psychology from the University of Kansas with a focus on school-based interventions, teacher training, and community-based services for high needs youth and their families. Her rewarding career has included international replication of evidence-based services for children and families engaged with child welfare systems, ju-*

venile justice, as well as domestic violence and violence prevention and children's mental health. Karen is internationally respected for her ground-breaking work, together with Dean Fixsen, in the area of implementation science and best practices.

# HOW TO USE THIS BOOK

As a parent (or caregiver of your teen), you can benefit from reading this entire book, or you can go to a chapter that addresses your specific concern. The specific Cake chapters represent metaphors for the most common situations I have helped teens and adults cope with for the last thirty years through my work as a counselor. If you suspect one of the Cake chapters (Rum Cake, Cupcakes, Pound Cake, etc.) applies to your teen, reading that chapter can assist in shedding some light on that situation. If you suspect something is not right with your teen but cannot put your finger on it, you may want to read all the Cake chapters to see if one resonates more directly with your concerns. Each Cake situation is typically more complex for any individual or family situation that is described in this book. There is a lot more to learn from each situation, so I encourage you to seek professional help when needed.

## Note on Gender Use

To avoid using one gender exclusively when referring to both male and female teens, I have used masculine and feminine pronouns throughout the book, recognizing that this choice does not fully reflect gender diversity. I do appreciate and honor the fact that there are teens who identify as transgender or who identify as non-binary. The chapters in this book are intended to be inclusive of diverse gender identities.

# DISCLAIMER

The personal stories I have shared are based on a compilation of clients and situations I have treated in my counseling practice. The identities and locations of these stories have been altered to protect the confidentiality of my clients.

Any advice given in this book should not be accepted as a substitute for the professional advice or treatment that a psychologist, psychiatrist, health-care provider, or licensed mental health counselor would give to an actual client in his or her care.

# PREFACE

As a licensed mental health counselor and middle and high school counselor, I have worked with thousands of teens and their parents over the past three decades which has led me to write this book. I want to provide parents with a resource for typical situations they will most likely encounter while raising their teens. Like most parents, as well as the professionals who are child and adolescent experts, I thought that there was a specific way (a recipe) to raise children, which would result in creating a successful adult. After all, there are thousands of parenting books on the shelves, vast research on child development, and, of course, advice from friends, family, and professionals focused on how to raise a healthy teen. However, that is not what the field, all the anecdotal evidence, or my own experience has taught me about raising teens. There is so much more.

This book is for parents who need a handbook for guidance when they do not feel they can turn to their friends and family for help. Often, parents feel embarrassed or helpless, feeling judged or blamed if they are having trouble raising their teen(s). They may feel isolated, wondering if friends and family will be critical, as if they are the reason for their teen's behaviors. *Is Raising Your Teen a Piece of Cake?* is a resource book—one that parents can thumb through to the chapter they need support with or read entirely for a more thorough understanding of the many situations most parents face when raising their teens. This book is intended to enlighten and inform parents about these situations for added support while parenting.

Comparing raising a teen to baking a cake is a bit of a stretch, but both involve the recipe you choose and the ingredients you add. Why not make these often frustrating and stressful years a bit more palatable by using cakes as metaphors for the parenting challenges you may face? I understand the ups and downs of raising teens, and I hope that these Cakes will shed some light and offer insight and support during the often turbulent teen years.

# PREP WORK

# 1

# IS RAISING YOUR TEEN
# A PIECE OF CAKE?

"Piece of Cake," I told my friend when she asked me about my experience raising my four teens. "Great experience, I would do it all over again if I could." In fact, raising my teens was often a combination of riding a roller coaster, herding cats, feeling pride, joy, embarrassment, humiliation, and straight-out panic and fear—not at all a piece of cake. Does this sound familiar? Is this your experience? Parents typically agree that, while they love their children, they would not want to revisit those teen years again. Many would agree they may be experiencing a form of post-traumatic stress as they look back on that stage of parenting.

What can a parent do to have a much more enjoyable and rewarding time while raising his or her teen? How can a parent raise his or her teen to have a positive attitude, be respectful, be successful, and make great choices? What does a parent need to do to raise a great kid? Are there specific techniques, styles, or skills that a parent needs?

Many parents have told me that having a teen who participates in sports, clubs, music programs, church, and any other positive experiences will keep him on a good path. Not only does a wholesome activity keep their teen busy learning and trying new experiences, but it can, also, help their teen develop his character by being a part of a team, becoming disciplined, managing time, acquiring new skills, gaining social confidence, and learning how to cope with loss or defeat. Keeping a teen active will hopefully steer him away from substance use or hanging out with the wrong crowd. Parents hope that this will result in a teen who makes good choices, has personal and professional success in life, has good self-esteem, and lives happily ever after. What more could a parent want? Unfortunately, for many of the parents I have worked with, this is not the case, especially during the teen years. Parents can feel scared, incompetent, and, even worse, humiliated and humbled by their teen's attitude and choices.

## IT IS NOT ALL ABOUT YOU ANYMORE

The adolescent years are a risky passage. Teens shift from being family focused to friend focused. These are their socially focused years, from finding a group they fit in with to participating in sports, clubs, and activities, exploring their own styles and identities, forming strong attractions and dating, and being connected through numerous social media sites. All these social activities become far more interesting than hanging out with their parents and siblings.

Your teen is a unique combination of DNA, his or her family, social environment, and, of course, his or her generation. Today's teen is at a complicated place in the history of adolescence. Due to the amount of information a teen can access today via the Internet and television, the transition from adolescent to an adult seems more blurred as kids have much more information than previous generations via these sources. The Internet and the wide range of television programs can expose teens to pornography, drugs, violence, and endless peering into the lives of teens and adults all around the world.

How does a caring, involved parent find the right recipe with the right ingredients to have a parenting experience that is a piece of cake?

There are many articles for raising a healthy teen on the Internet and many good books on parenting your adolescent. Many have good suggestions for raising teens; however, when it comes to your teen, there is no perfect fit for each situation you may face. Having worked with thousands of teens and parents over thirty years, I have learned there is simply no method, philosophy, training, skill set, or body of research that will fit every teen. Every parent, teen, and situation is unique.

I want parents to do the best they can, with what they know, while realizing that almost all parents will run into unwanted ingredients and unexpected circumstances that will complicate their attempts to raise their teen the way they thought was best. The Cake chapters describe these added ingredient situations so that you can learn more about your teen and then be better prepared to cope with these often-turbulent years.

## WHAT CAN YOU DO AS A PARENT?

Your teen is unique. If you are raising several children, then you already know that each one is different. Each teen you raise will result in a different parenting experience. How could there possibly be one recipe that tells you how to raise your unique teen?

The ingredients that go into raising your teen: love, safety, care, activities, events, schooling, discipline, guidance, wisdom, religious and spiritual beliefs, techniques, skills, and any others you have added, may result in the surprising revelation that there are no reliable formulas, skills, or techniques that will produce the teen you hoped you would be raising. There is no predicting, no correlation, no causation, and no guarantee that what you do as a parent while raising your child will result in the outcomes you want for your teen. This book addresses what you can do when you face *unwanted* ingredients and need help coping with them.

This book, *Is Raising Your Teen a Piece of Cake?* will describe many common situations that you as a parent may face when parenting. For example, Rum Cake, which will help you recognize and navigate the situation if you find out your teen has been drinking; Having Your Cake And Not Eating It, Too, discusses eating disorders, and Carrot Cake will help you recognize that not all behaviors are equally serious. Hopefully, by educating yourself about these situations, you will not feel as alone or fearful of these years. Instead, you will hopefully realize that these situations can be common (as stressful as they are) and that most can end as being a part of your teen's past, not his or her future. Even though you may have set a solid foundation for your child, the teen years can bring many unwelcome surprises that result in stress and frustration for the entire family.

## BAKING YOUR CAKE

By using the analogy that raising a teen can be like baking a cake, *Is Raising Your Teen a Piece of Cake?* assumes that your style of parenting, your philosophy, your values and beliefs, your skills, and your background and life lessons will be the ingredients you will most likely use while baking your cake. When you follow your recipe and use your ingredients, you are hopeful your teen will turn out the way you would like. Not only do you need ingredients to make a good cake, but you will also need a pan to bake it in. Think of your teen's home as the pan—a place that can provide safety, security, nourishment, guidance, boundaries, and, of course, love.

Stir your ingredients, pour them into your pan, and then set the oven to the correct temperature to bake your cake. Think of the oven as the outside environment that influences the pan. Other influences can reset the temperature: schools, church, clubs, sports, organizations, relatives, the Internet, social media, television, movies, books, neighborhood, and, of course, friends and peers. You place your cake in the oven. You have followed your personal recipe, chosen the ingredients, and your cake begins to bake. At this point, you have very little control, no matter how well you followed your recipe. As it bakes, you are not guaranteed that your cake is going to turn out according to your desires.

You could have a cake that is too dry or too moist or one that does not taste as good as it should. Or unfortunately, it could fall and end up ruined. How can this happen? There are so many variables that impact the outcome, even with the best recipes and ingredients.

Is baking a cake the same as parenting a teen? Of course not, your teen is a person,  parenting is complicated, and, in comparison, baking a cake is simple. However, using this analogy will keep things a bit lighter, even though many of the issues are not light; in fact, some can be life-threatening. However, raising a teen is like baking a cake because, ultimately, no matter how you raise your teen (the ingredients you put in), where you raise your teen (the pan), and the life your teen lives outside of your home (the oven), all will impact your teen. Because there are so many variables (only some of which you can control) your teen's experiences can result in some unpredictable outcomes.

*Is Raising Your Teen a Piece of Cake?* will provide helpful advice and information for raising a successful teen. Each Cake chapter will give you a closer look at some of the specialty cakes. The Specialty Cakes in these chapters are organized under: Harmful, Secret, Special, Surprise, and Lighter ingredients, all of which can cause stress and anxiety, especially since many were not the ingredients *you* added when raising your teen. Unfortunately, these are often typical situations for teens. As a parent, you may face one of them or many of them. Or you may be one of the fortunate few who has the lighter ingredients and skim right by the teen years unscathed.

> **The main point I want to emphasize is that no matter what foundation you give your children in their early years, no matter how much effort or how many opportunities you provided, and no matter how much love and support you give, you simply cannot predict your teen's path. Will it be safe, without detours and collisions, or smooth or bumpy?**

The bottom line is that you have to do the best you can with the recipe and ingredients you choose. When other outside influences get added as unwanted ingredients, parents and teens often reach out for other means of support: the Internet, friends' and families' advice and professional help. As painful as many of these situations are, you are not alone; most parents are not equipped to navigate these years without extra support. Often parents feel shame and guilt, as they blame themselves and think that family, friends, coworkers, teachers, and neighbors are judging them for their teens' behaviors. I wrote this book to remind you while you do not have control over *all* the ingredients you do have control over *how* you deal with them. I hope that these chapters will enlighten and equip you with insight and suggestions for helping you and your teen successfully navigate the adolescent passage.

# 2

# FIVE RECIPE TIPS

## 1. STAYING CALM AND COLLECTED

The teen years are some of the most frustrating years you will navigate. Your frustration can turn you into a frazzled and sometimes frantic parent. You could find yourself yelling, swearing at your teen, putting her down, calling her names, threatening her, throwing her things, putting her friends down, making accusations before you know the facts, and assuming the worst of her, behaving in ways you never thought you would. All of these behaviors can interfere with raising a respectful and successful teen.

Yelling turns your volume up so loud that your teen will either duck for cover instead of hearing the message you are sending or will yell back to overpower you. Instead, remind yourself to stay calm, use "I" messages ("I am so angry, frustrated, overwhelmed, stressed, tired of this" and so on). If you can avoid swearing at your daughter, chances are she will also avoid swearing at you and other adults in her life. Putting your teen down, such as "Look at your room; you are a lazy slob and are never going to amount to anything," will not motivate her to suddenly want to clean her room. Angrily throwing out her clothes or possessions will not motivate her either.

If you are not happy with her friends, it is better to let her know your concerns instead of directly putting them down. "Your friend is a stoner; I don't trust her," is an example of what to avoid. Your teen is very sensitive about her friends and will defend them if you put them down. Instead, let her know you are concerned about her friend. "I worry Jenny is using drugs, and I am not happy she dropped out of school. She isn't a friend I think is a good influence on you. What do you think? Are you, also, spending time with your other friends?"

While it is true that your teen can hide many of her behaviors from you, do not be overly suspicious of her choices. Extend some trust and let her know you are confident she will make good choices and use her head. If you do find she is doing everything *but* making good choices and using her head; then be vigilant about what she is up to and give her consequences. Teens get worn down when their parents always accuse them of being up to something.

It is easy to escalate your temper when dealing with teen behavior, so avoid making any threats, giving consequences, or demanding change until you time yourself out, calm down, and think more rationally.

## 2. PRACTICE IMPROVISATION

Love and parenting come in many forms. Not all parents are five-star chefs when it comes to adding all the ingredients needed to parent. Some have never picked up a spatula or bowl in their lives. Some went to gourmet cooking school. Most are somewhere in between. However, as parents all of you share one powerful experience: you love your kids and want the best for them! No matter your age or experience when you are raising your teen, you are in the company of all parents who share this common denominator: all parents want their teens to be happy, make good choices, and have great lives. Do your best with what you know. You will not always get it right; you will make mistakes, have regrets, run out of answers, and at times, be utterly exhausted. You are not alone. You share the company of every parent navigating the teen years. If you can remember to throw in some fun and lighten up these parenting years for both you and your teen, that would be a welcome ingredient among the stressful ups and downs of the teen years!

When I was in high school, my best friend's dad asked her to come into the kitchen so he could talk to her. She moaned and groaned as she got up from our very intense teen conversation to see what he wanted. When she went into the kitchen, he met her by smashing a cream pie in her face! She was startled, of course, then everyone started laughing. My family seemed so serious and yet her family was fun! So, throw in some fun. She may balk or have a fit, but she also may give you some points (underneath her scowl) for being playful.

## 3. IT IS NOT ALL ABOUT YOU

While it may seem that you are in the driver's seat, you are not the only one raising your teen. Other people impact your teen's life: teachers, relatives, siblings, coaches, clergy, bosses, friends, and peers. And don't forget the negative impact of challenging life experiences: losing friends, having health challenges, adjusting to a new home or environment, experiencing divorce, being rejected in relationships, stressors from school, not making the sports team, coping with family financial worries, the list goes on and on.

Your child can probably access the web and apps with more skill and finesse than you can. Teens are accessing and processing information much faster than any other generation to date. They can see violence and pornography and participate in chats from all types of websites. My teen once said to me, "Mom, you cannot go to that website; it is too terrible!" and yet, she was visiting it at the age of seventeen.

You put in all the ingredients you feel are best, hoping for a predictable outcome as you raise your teen. However, there are a vast number of influences that impact your teen's choices, attitudes, and experiences. All those outside influences will affect how your teen turns out. It is not always about you.

## 4. BE YOU, EVEN WHEN YOU HAVE NO IDEA WHAT TO DO

Be real and authentic with your teen instead of all-knowing. Just because you read the hottest parenting book on the market or watched an episode of Dr. Phil and learned some new ideas, does not mean that you are going to get it right. Teens know when you are managing them with a new strategy.

Avoid using, phrases or buzzwords that you got from a best-selling author such as "We are using tough love, son." This comes across as scripted, and teens have little tolerance when they think you are parenting from a book. Your teen could care less about your referencing this; all he cares about is what the consequence will mean to his life. Instead, point out that you are not an expert when it comes to being a parent and you are doing the best you can with what you know.

> **Tell him that you are going to do everything you can to keep him healthy and safe. Let him know that your love for him results in worrying about him, wanting to protect him and that you will set expectations and boundaries because you come from two central emotional positions: love and fear.**

You have every right to parent your teen, make mistakes, not always do the right thing, and give consequences as needed. You are trying to keep your teen safe, continue to let him know that it is your responsibility to keep him safe and on a good path. Pay attention to as much as you can, and at the same time, realize that you are not omnipresent.

Sometimes we think that sharing stories with our teen about our teen years, such as when we tried alcohol, had our first relationship and took risks, is a way to help him. It is best to save the "when I was your age…"

stories for when your son or daughter is older (over twenty-one) and well into adulthood. Unfortunately, he is more likely to interpret your stories as permission to try new behaviors (since you did), so try to keep the focus on him, not you.

## 5. GIVE YOURSELF A BREAK. THIS IS NOT EASY!

It is perfectly fine to read books, take parenting classes, and seek guidance and support from friends, relatives, and other professionals while raising your teen. You were not born with a spatula in your hand. It can be helpful and comforting to learn about all of the various ingredients that go into raising your teen. Educating yourself about the stage of adolescence and parenting can help you navigate and feel normal during the times you might otherwise feel lost and dazed.

> However, if your teen does not follow the path you imagined, cut yourself some slack. You did your best with what you knew, the resources you had to work with, and the circumstances and situations that came into their life.

You love your kids, and you probably love cake; both are enjoyable when everything turns out just right. The truth is that both will turn out exactly as they are going to, no matter what ingredients you add or what recipe you follow. There are just some things in life that we cannot control. Remember the curve balls you threw to your parents? You have come a long way from your own teen years. At some point, we all grow up, pay the bills, and become adults faced with all the responsibilities that come with navigating life's ups and downs. Relax, use your humor, take good care of yourself, and remind yourself that this, too, shall pass.

# 3

# BAKE FROM SCRATCH
# OR A MIX?

## FROM SCRATCH

Some of you will be raising your teen from scratch. You believe that the best you can give your kids is being at home and personally looking after them 24-7.

During her infant and toddler years, you put your daughter to bed at a decent hour for a good night's sleep. You cuddled her, rocked her, held her, sang to her, fed her, changed her diapers, and dressed her. Throughout the day, you kept her safe; made sure she got enough playtime, exercise, and needed rest; exposed her to learning; and did all the other millions of things parents do every day to care for their kids.

When she was in her elementary school years, you woke her up in time to dress for school and eat breakfast, made her lunch, and you walked her to the school or bus stop, or you drove her yourself. After school, you were home for her, or you might have picked her up from school each day. You provided snacks after school, you checked in on her homework, and often you provided the transportation for all the places she needed to be. You drove her to various sports activities, dance classes, music lessons, and friends' homes.

While she was at school, perhaps, you worked from home, cleaned, planned dinner, shopped for groceries, ran errands, worked out at the gym, went shopping, spent time on your computer, and maybe even had lunch with a friend. You checked the calendar to know where everyone needed to be and when; coordinating the family calendar to minimize chaos and often getting everyone back late in the evening. Your days were busy and often exhausting from full-time parenting.

When you got out for some "me time," you might have enjoyed a book club, a yoga class or a girls' night out. You might have attended a parenting class or two. You might have been busy with volunteer work at your child's school, PTA, or church activities. You might have volunteered to go on field trips, helped to supervise skate parties, been the team mom, and attended numerous sporting events. You attended all parent conferences. You kept your daughter's homework and assignments in check. You knew all her teachers. You advocated for her. You gave her the necessary consequences if she started sliding. You may have taken fitness classes, worked out at the gym, or enjoyed outdoor walks or runs. Your life was busy, and you wondered how parents working outside the home managed it all.

Some of you may have added church to your family life, being sure your daughter attended church and participated in opportunities to hang out with other teens from the youth group. You gave your daughter lots of opportunities: travel, skiing, camps for sports, or other interests. Fashion-wise, she always had what she needed to be sure she was not committing "social suicide." You did everything possible to put in every ingredient to make your Cake from scratch.

> And, all this work, dedication, effort, time, and attention to detail may or may not have rewarded you with the intended outcome! Your daughter may or may not turn out as you expected. All that attention to detail, all that work to cook from scratch, and still

your Cake may fall. Or, maybe devoting all your time to choosing the right ingredients and your belief that the best Cakes are made from scratch did pay off. If there is one predictable outcome when raising your child, it is that there is no predictable outcome when raising your child.

You get to choose what works best for you and what you believe to be the best care for your family. You then implement your own style of parenting. It is your personal choice of how you will raise your kids. However, no matter what you do, you cannot guarantee a specific outcome. This can cause great anguish and guilt, second-guessing yourself, or wondering what you did wrong.

If you are not getting the results you are looking for while raising your teen, avoid blaming yourself. Instead, give yourself some grace that you are doing the best you can, are parenting according to your beliefs and values, are coping with and navigating the unexpected, and are often sacrificing your own needs to be there for your teen.

## CHOOSING A MIX

Perhaps you would rather buy the cake mix than go to all that time and trouble to make a cake from scratch. You love your kids just as much as parents who cook from scratch; however, you work outside the home and manage your home life with your work life. If you are a single parent or need the income to support your family, or you simply love to work, you will be parenting just as well as the from scratch parent, but, perhaps, with more efficiency. Your child will spend time in daycare, with nannies, or with family or friends who care for him while you work. Maybe you could not make it to every game or performance your son was involved in, but you did your best to get to as many as possible. Perhaps, your career demanded a majority of your time and attention. Cake-mix parents love a delicious cake as much as anyone; however, their schedules may have prohibited them from being there in the morning to be sure their son gets off to school. You may have called or sent him a text from work to be sure he was up and moving. You may have sent your son off to school with a homemade lunch, or maybe you bought a month's worth of school lunches. And after school, your son got himself home while you were still at work.

Once you returned home after a stressful day of work and commuting, you attended to the hustle and bustle of getting dinner ready and your son off to sports and activities. This may have meant a quick drive-through at the local fast food restaurant. You checked in on your son's homework and grades but may not have had as much time to micromanage as the make-from-scratch parent. Cake mix parents are just as capable as the make-from-scratch parents; both types put in the ingredients for raising a healthy and successful teen: love, time, care, protection, guidance, boundaries, expectations, supervision, celebration, support, and consequences when needed.

And yet, your teen, just like the teen from scratch, is going to turn out exactly like he or she is going to turn out! Your teen will either be a source of immense pride, possible disappointment, and grief, or a combination of all. All teens have their own unique ingredients no matter what mix was chosen.

No matter how you choose to parent, to stay home or to work, there is no right way or wrong way to raise your teen. The only way is what you believe to be best, the ingredients you choose to care for your child. Parenting is the toughest job in the world, and parenting your teen during adolescence will be more challenging than at any other stage of your child's development. All the seeds you plant, the home life you build, the love and care you give your teen is the best you can do.

When you talk to your successful friends about their childhoods, I bet many of them had a rough ride. Their parents may have done the best they could, and many may have fallen short or were excellent at parenting. Their childhood does not seem to impact how successful their adult lives are. I am not downplaying or minimizing childhood abuse or neglect and their impact and trauma on a human being. I am saying that I have learned, by my experiences of working with teens from foster care to the best of families, that the choices teens make are not directly correlated with how they are raised. Even though parents blame themselves if their teen is making bad choices, or is depressed, suicidal, or seemingly not happy, the truth is that parents and a teen's family life provide only some of the ingredients. Many other factors impact a human being's choices, attitudes, view of life, and wellbeing.

> **All the love and care you give, the sacrifices you make, raising your child by staying home or by working, are essential, but are not the only factors that influence the life they choose to lead. It is not all about you; it is about more than you.**

# 4

# MY CAKE FELL!

All parents are going to face situations when the cake they were baking falls or turns out much differently than the recipe intended. These are situations where the teen may add her own ingredients to the mix. Or the parents end up adding ingredients they had never foreseen or planned (such as divorce). There are so many situations that parents can face during the teen years that can be heartbreaking, stressful, worrisome, and even dangerous. The teen years can be a very turbulent ride for everyone, because of the nature of adolescents; the tendency to take more risks, to want so badly to fit in, and to exercise the freedom they now have (especially during the driving years). With all the opportunities they are exposed to, the temptations to try things parents have clearly warned them about, and all the other influences during these years add up to uncertainty about how all of this will turn out.

## THERE IS SIMPLY NO PREDICTING

The next chapters will focus on all the different cakes a parent could end up baking. When parents are facing difficult situations with their teen, they may find it embarrassing to share with family and friends what they are going through. They may feel they will be judged or that they are bad parents, or that it is their fault. Hopefully, these chapters can shed some light on what you and many other parents may be facing. Families are often overwhelmed or embarrassed by these situations and keep them secret, not always knowing whom to turn to for help. It is important to remember that no matter what ingredients you have put into raising your child, all the right ones, all the wrong ones, or a mixture of both, you simply cannot predict how your teen will turn out.

I have worked with thousands of teens and their families throughout my career. I have worked with teens from foster care who have had extremely tough circumstances during their childhoods that have left them hurt and scarred. I have witnessed these often abused and neglected teens very deliberately making excellent choices throughout their teen years. They refrain from drugs and alcohol, strive to get good grades, are respectful, and are involved in many healthy activities such as school clubs, church activities, and sports. I have also seen teens from foster care go in another direction. It is not predictable.

The same thing can happen in healthy and intact families. Teens can gravitate toward alcohol and drugs, get involved in the wrong peer groups, be attracted to a very unhealthy and abusive relationship, shoplift, get failing grades, have angry, defiant attitudes toward parents or other adults. They can get suspended from school, get driving citations, end up in court with a probation officer, get pregnant, and experience other heartbreaking and stressful situations for the entire family. Or, your teen can breeze through adolescence, making great choices, without these risks. It is, unfortunately, unpredictable.

> **I suggest that you should focus on being the best parent you can be. I also suggest that you ought to give yourself a break when it comes to taking on the guilt, shame, and blame when your teen does not turn out like you thought he would. You can only do the best you can. No one has a perfect childhood (or life, for that matter). No one has an ideal set of parenting skills that produce a**

perfect teen. Every teen will face his own unique set of circumstances, with his own unique DNA and his own unique family and
social situations. There is no single recipe.

You are not alone. You are not to blame. The parents who have made the
worst mistakes, the parents who have done almost everything well and the
parents who come in between all share one common denominator: no matter
how they parented, they cannot always count on their teen turning out how
they intended. You can control your behavior, your own mental and physical
well-being, you can use your support systems and do the best you can with
your knowledge, skills, and discernment. You can provide a loving and safe
home, and you can make good decisions about how you parent and how you
support your self and your teen. When needed you can change course, learn
new parenting skills, adjust some of the ways you parent to get better results
and stay committed to supporting your teen through their adolescence. You
do have a tremendous influence on how your teen feels, acts and the choices
he makes. Unfortunately, there can be those unwanted ingredients that can
surprise you, resulting in stress and anxiety as you parent your teen.

# HARMFUL
# INGREDIENTS

NOT FOR CONSUMPTION

# 5

# RUM CAKE

## ALCOHOL USE

John and Kate came to see me when they could no longer figure out what to do about their sixteen-year-old son, Brian. They described him as using drugs, disregarding their rules, coming and going as he pleased, and recently, he was kicked out of school. I asked what made them think that he was using drugs and alcohol. Kate was thoughtful for a moment, then leaned forward.

"Well, nowadays it's a pretty common occurrence for me to come into his room and find bottles of vodka or empty cans of beer. He comes home smelling like weed, oh and on Wednesday, John found a vape pen and a pipe in his backpack."

"When you found the drugs, did you ask Brian about it?"

"Yes. When John found the vape pen we came into his room to address it but, Brian's face got all red and scary, and he screamed in our faces, 'Don't mess with my stuff!'"

John nodded and spoke. "All he wants to do now is go hang out with this group of kids who kind of scare me. They don't have parents who are involved, or the parents are using drugs themselves, so they can party anytime they want. He doesn't even see his old friends from his soccer team anymore."

"Have you tried to sit down and talk to him, to find out what is going on with him? To see if something might be bothering him?"

John continued, "All the time. In fact, I tried to talk to him three days ago, like, really talk to him. We had grounded him because we found him sneaking out in the middle of the night to go hang out with this kid who is in and out of juvenile hall. Anyway, I wanted to talk to him about the choices he was making, and how he was speaking to his teachers and being disrespectful, about him punching a hole in the bathroom wall, and he just stared at me and told me that I didn't understand him, that I never would and that he hated me."

"Was he always like this, kind of oppositional defiant? That's where you see a pattern of wanting to do the opposite of what you want. For example, has he always argued with you a lot or been defiant to you or other authority figures?"

"No that's why we are so confused. Two and a half years ago he was an "A" student. He played soccer, he loved science and math, he used to come downstairs and cook dinner with me, and he and John used to stay up late together watching movies. It's almost like someone took our Brian and left us this other kid."

John sighed. "We are exhausted and sad. It feels like we've tried everything. Everything."

As I got to know John and Kate more, I was impressed with the lives they had built. John was a well-respected family physician and Kate was a beloved first-grade teacher. They lived in a small resort community with a quaint downtown and one of the country's largest recreational lakes. They were involved caring parents to their two younger children, an adopted ten-year-old son who was flourishing in school, and an eight-year-old daughter who played two instruments and loved ballet. They attended church often and, every summer they loved to take family vacations their kids enjoyed. By all accounts, they had created a stable, warm, and loving home.

As a counselor, I am trained to look deeper, to explore with the family to see if I can locate any emotional or physical abuse, alcohol or drug addiction, or any indicator that the private life of a family may be contributing to their teen's acting-out behaviors.

I began by meeting with Brian, who agreed to meet me for two sessions. I also met with their two younger children. I could locate no hidden addiction or physical or emotional abuse. What I did discover was that Brian had been adopted at six months old and his early start in life had been pretty rough. His biological mother was an addict and he had been in foster care since birth. I figured out that he most likely had a diagnosis of RAD (reactive attachment disorder, see glossary). RAD is a disorder that can begin in infancy and reveal itself fully later in a child's life. It can look like withdrawal, sadness or irritability, shying away from comfort, or not asking for support when it is offered. His RAD and his addiction issues were causing him to want to run away from home. He seemed only to come home when he needed a shower, food, and rest. Then he was out the window or door again.

Brian continued to ignore his parents' very reasonable rules, the same standards by which their other well-adjusted children were living. I counseled John and Kate to be more consistent with the boundaries they set for Brian, as they tended to let him walk all over them. Often their response was, "We just want to love him; we don't want to push him away."

Eventually, after several minor skirmishes with the police, Brian was arrested for possession of cocaine and charged with a felony. Much to the embarrassment and pain of John and Kate, neighbors would peer out of their windows when the police

**would show up. John and Kate found it humiliating when they assumed people were judging them for some hidden dysfunction looming in their beautiful home.**

**John and Kate were hurt by Brian's defiant behaviors, hurtful words, and utter rejection of them and their way of life. They had created a loving, secure home with a highly supportive extended family and friends. In essence, John and Kate had put in all the right ingredients as they raised Brian. They had done everything they were supposed to do as devoted, loving parents. Yet in the end, much of how Brian turned out was not within their control. We worked together to discover what they could control in their lives and how they could continue to nurture themselves and their other two children.**

This is a family who had put in all the right ingredients, from wanting children so badly they adopted (and then, as is often the case, Kate delivered a healthy girl a few years later) to creating a loving, secure home with extended family and friends who have also loved and supported their kids. They are devastated and feel guilty, wondering what they did wrong. They are hurt by their son's angry words, defiant behaviors, and utter rejection of them, and they feel helpless. They know much of his behaviors are addiction-related, but they cannot force him to go to treatment. They are wondering if he will go back to school in the fall, as he would be a senior, but since he was suspended the last semester of his junior year, he has a lot of catching up to do. The entire situation is heartbreaking and certainly not the outcome John and Kate had ever expected while adopting and raising their kids. Navigating his addictions and the juvenile justice system, hearing the mean comments he says to them, and having holes punched in their walls was never the life that John and Kate had envisioned.

## YOUR TEEN AND ALCOHOL

If you suspect your teen is drinking, or you have caught him with alcohol, intoxicated, or you know he had been drinking at a party, it can feel very scary. And, at the same time, you could put it in the denial box with thoughts such as "OK, this is upsetting, but I drank as a kid. I know teens drink, so this is just a normal thing," or "I knew that James was a bad influence. I will make sure my son does not hang with him any longer!" You love your child, you have protected him, and you thought he was pretty innocent, especially since his grades are good and he plays football and track. There is an athletic code, and you knew your teen would honor it to not jeopardize being on the team. However, you now have news or evidence that your teen is drinking.

Parents often do not seek my professional help until there are more detrimental consequences related to their teen's drinking. The parents who come to me are typically dealing with a teen with a bad attitude, defiant, moody, often going out with friends on the weekends to party or drink and then sleeping in on the weekends, hung over, unmotivated, and irritable. Grades can start to drop, or the police notified parents that their teen was given a MIP (Minor in Possession) or MUI (Minor Under the Influence). In one of my worst cases, a young man had driven home from a party with two people in the car, lost control on a curve, and killed the front-seat passenger, his cousin. He ended up in my office as he was very depressed and suicidal, completely freaked out about his future and deeply saddened that all of this was his fault. His parents insisted that he see me, as his risk for suicide was high. This is, of course, the nightmare that parents dread; drinking and driving. Your teen may be smart enough not to combine the two, but since alcohol affects judgment, your teen could end up thinking he was OK enough to drive or could get in the car with someone else who has been drinking.

A lot depends on the situation when it comes to dealing with your teen's drinking and his age. If you catch your teen drinking from the ages of 13-15, you still have a lot of parental control and can intervene. Your teen is usually under your roof, and most of his rides involve you. This gives you the power to know where your teen is most of the time, and you can check to see if you smell alcohol on him or observe if he is acting unusual.

Talking to your teen about when he started drinking, with whom, and where, will give you useful information to curtail future opportunities. Discussing how harmful alcohol is (there is plenty of information on the internet and in this chapter regarding the risks) may help, though teens often have the attitude that nothing bad can happen to them. Seeking a drug and alcohol center for an assessment and then treatment is always a good idea. Whatever your teen is reporting ("I only drank once!") is usually an attempt to fool you, so multiply at least by five. Teens typically underreport, no matter how sincere they seem.

If your teen is older, 16-18, you have a lot less influence, especially if he is driving. A car is your teen's "first apartment," and he can now come and go, as he pleases, to unsupervised households (and just because parents are home does not mean there is any supervision) and to parties. Teens can sneak alcohol just about anywhere for any occasion: sports events, dances, sleepovers, parks, movies, you name it. A teen can find a way.

## WHAT YOU CAN DO

You still have a lot you can do to address your teen's drinking, and it is far better to address this issue than to minimize it ("typical teen behavior," such as "I used to drink and party as a teen, and I am fine," etc.).

You do not have to have all the right words to be upfront with your teen about their drinking. You can stay in your parental power, which is what you do have influence and control over. "There is no underage drinking allowed in this home, period. When you no longer live here, and you are out on your own, you can do whatever you want, but not under my roof." "I am getting you an appointment with a drug and alcohol counselor for an assessment." (Believe me, when you say this he will have a huge push back: "I do not need any assessment, I am fine, I can quit drinking whenever I want, this is not a problem, you are making too big of a deal out of all this.") However, if your drinking teen is driving, suspending driving privileges until he has an assessment and complies with treatment recommendations, is well within your control. Once you feel more confident he is not drinking (and you continue to monitor him the best you can) you may then choose to trust him again to use the car.

Not letting him spend the night with friends is another effective intervention, as most drinking will occur out of your sight. However, at the same time, let him know if he is drinking away from home, he is not to drive or get into a car with someone else who is drinking. Let him know that he can call and you will either come and pick him up, or he can spend the night there. Safety is the biggest concern, of course. Driving under the influence and drinking too much (i.e., alcohol poisoning) are the two most dangerous situations for your teen.

**Teens will be very tempted to try alcohol, and it can be readily available via friends or stealing from parents. Some teens have no interest for many reasons and get through their high school years without a drop. But many others do succumb to drinking so not addressing it is far worse than the tension that erupts when you do confront your teen. When your son knows you know, the sneaking part lessens as he knows you are suspicious and will be watching him more closely.**

When you find out that your teen is drinking, it is a wake-up call. You are now aware that your teen is no longer innocent, that he is choosing behaviors and getting away with them, which means he has been lying and sneaking around, breaking your trust. It is typical to make risky choices when you are a teen. There are many reasons for making these choices: underdeveloped brain development (see Dr. Siegel's research on this in the Glossary), genetic predisposition linked to alcoholism, and peer pressure, to name a few. The most important thing when dealing with this *is* dealing with this, not ignoring it or rationalizing it is a normal adolescent stage. The attention and support you give your teen will be the best thing you can do because it is often the only thing you can do. Sadly, in some cases, everything you do will not stop your teen, who may continue to drink and could have a lifelong problem. However, on the positive side, your early intervention may help your teen make better choices, and the support he gets provides him with the education, skills, and motivation he needs to stay away from drinking.

## THIS IS MORE SERIOUS THAN YOU MAY WANT TO THINK

Teens may be experimenting with alcohol, some as early as preteens and many by the time they are ready to graduate. Studies show that by age fifteen, half of all teens have had at least one drink. By age eighteen, more than 70 percent of teens have had at least one drink.[1] Throughout their school years, teens' resistance to abstain decreases, and the peer pressure increases. Older teens, now equipped with a driver's license, are free to visit friends and find the parties, and many times, parents are misled as to where they are or what they are doing.

Alcohol is the drug of choice among America's adolescents, used more than tobacco or illicit drugs.[2] Many teens are experiencing the consequences of excessive drinking at an early age. As a result, underage drinking is a leading public health problem in the United States.[3]

---

1 "Underage Drinking," National Institute of Alcohol Abuse and Alcoholism, accessed April 30th 2019, https://www.niaaa.nih.gov/underage-drinking-0.
2 "Underage Drinking," National Institute of Health, Accessed April 30th, 2019, https://report.nih.gov/NIHfactsheets/ViewFactSheet.aspx?csid=21.
3 "Brochures and Fact Sheets," National Institute of Health, Accessed April 30th, 2019, http://pubs.niaaa.nih.gov/publications.

Once your teen tries alcohol, there is no predicting where this is going or how it is going to turn out. Will he experiment a bit, use it every once in a while, or begin a lifetime problem of drinking or alcoholism? Parents often tolerate their teen's use of alcohol by justifying it: "Well, at least he's not into drugs!" However, alcohol can be one of the most life-threatening and dangerous drugs a teen can use.

## THE RISKS

Following are many of the risks associated with underage drinking:

Death—4,358 people under age twenty-one die each year from alcohol-related car crashes, homicides, suicides, alcohol poisoning, and other injuries such as falls, burns, and drowning.

School problems—such as higher absence and poor or failing grades.

Social problems—such as fighting and lack of participation in youth activities.

Legal problems—such as arrest for driving or physically hurting someone while drunk.

Physical problems—such as hangovers or illnesses.

Sexual activity—unwanted, unplanned, and unprotected sexual activity.

Developmental problems—disruption of normal growth and sexual development.

**Assault**—physical and sexual assault.

**Emotional problems**—higher risk for suicide and homicide.

**Accidents and injuries**—alcohol-related car crashes and other unintentional injuries, such as burns, falls and drowning.

**Memory problems**

**Drugs**—abuse of other drugs.

**Brain development**—changes in brain development that may have lifelong effects.

**Poisoning**—death from alcohol poisoning. [4]

Teens often drink with friends or at parties. Drinking multiple shots of hard alcohol is the rage these days, which is the fast track to getting intoxicated, passing out, alcohol poisoning, and possible death. On average, young people have about five drinks on a single occasion, which can be considered binge drinking. The National Institute on Alcohol Abuse and Alcoholism (NIAAA) defines binge drinking as a pattern of drinking alcohol that brings blood alcohol concentration (BAC) to 0.08 g/dL This typically occurs after four drinks for women and five drinks for men—in about 2 hours.[5]

Frequent binge drinkers (nearly one million high-school students nationwide) are more likely to engage in risky behaviors, including using other drugs such as marijuana and cocaine, having sex with six or more partners, and earning grades that are mostly Ds and Fs in school.[6] Girls are particular-

---

4 "Facts sheet Underage Drinking," Centers for Disease Control and Prevention, accessed April 30th, 2019, http://www.cdc.gov/alcohol/fact-sheets/underage-drinking.htm.

5 "Drinking Levels Defined," National Institute of Health, accessed April 30th, 2019, https://www.niaaa.nih.gov/alcohol-health/overview-alcohol-consumption/moderate-binge-drinking.

6 "Alcohol Alert, "accessed April 30th", 2019, National Institute of Health, accessed April 30th, 2019. http://pubs.niaaa.nih.gov/publications/AA67/AA67.htm.

ly vulnerable when drinking or being around boys who are drinking. Girls can be date-raped and may not remember what happened after a bout of drinking.

The younger the age when someone begins drinking alcohol, the more likely he or she will have a lifelong problem. Doctors selected the age of twenty-one as the age that a person's body may be able to absorb alcohol without interfering with brain and body development. Teens who start drinking early increase their risks of a lifelong addiction, being in unsafe situations, or ending up in outpatient or inpatient facilities. Young people who start drinking before the age of fifteen are four times more likely to develop alcohol dependence during their lifetime than those who began drinking at age twenty-one or later. A parent with a history of alcoholism also contributes to the risk of developing alcoholism.[7]

### WARNING SIGNS THAT YOUR TEEN MAY BE DRINKING

- Changes in mood, including anger and irritability
- Academic or behavioral problems in school
- Rebelliousness
- Changing groups of friends
- Low energy level
- Less interest in activities or care in appearance
- Finding alcohol among your teen's things
- Smelling alcohol on their breath
- Problems concentrating or remembering
- Slurred speech
- Coordination problems

7 "Underage Drinking, " National Institute of Health, accessed April 30th, 2019, https://www.niaaa.nih.gov/underage-drinking-0.

## YES, YOU CAN DO SOMETHING TO HELP YOUR TEEN!

Take action! It is OK to search his room, backpack, or car, scan his social media accounts, read his text messages, and search for evidence of drinking. You do not need to tell your son you looked through his things because he will make the issue all about your snooping instead of his drinking. Your son is your legal responsibility until he is eighteen and independent. As long as he is under the age of eighteen and dependent on you for shelter, money, and food, you absolutely can be vigilant about checking for any clues you may find that point to drinking. Typically, asking your son if he is drinking or having a problem with alcohol will only result in lying and defensive behavior. Most will not admit it unless caught, and most parents want to believe their teens have not added rum to the cake mix.

Swift and immediate action, however, is required. Talk to your son, talk to a drug and alcohol counselor, and/or get the advice of a health care professional. Be sure your alcohol is locked up to avoid the temptation of your son taking your alcohol. Take away his driving privileges if you think he has ever driven after drinking. In some cases, get your son to an outpatient group, Alateen, or inpatient treatment. You still have influence over him at this age, and these resources can educate him about the risks of alcohol while he is young. Listening to other professionals or peers about their drinking in a recovery group will often be more influential than what you tell him as a parent.

## IS THIS MY FAULT? DID I MISS SOMETHING?

One of the most important messages I want you to grasp, and digest is that you are only a small slice of the cake when it comes to all of the influences that impact your teen's choices. Your son is a product of his genetic coding, social influences, opportunities, peers, television, movies, commercials, etc. So, no, this isn't your fault.

Parents ask me, "Do you have to stop drinking around your teen to send a positive message?" There is no direct correlation between parents' drinking and their teen's drinking. Some teens raised in families where one or both parents are alcoholics will refuse to drink based on what they have experienced. At the other end of the spectrum are parents who do not touch alcohol, and yet their teen sneaks behind their backs to drink with friends. A teen from any family life situation can experiment and abuse alcohol. However, because drinking is so prevalent in our society and teens observe adults drinking at home, restaurants, television, movies, commercials, sports events, concerts, etc., they are already being programmed to drink, because that is what the majority of adults do.[8]

Teens are looking for independence, new challenges, and are risk takers as they often feel they are immune from being harmed. Many want to try alcohol but often do not consider the impact on their behavior and health or other consequences. Teens drink for many reasons. Some give in to peer pressure, some are just curious, and some are managing stress. The pressure of teens' social and school life, hectic schedules, personal insecurities or anxiety, and relationship issues all add up to stress. Ending up at a weekend party or a friend's home that gives them access to alcohol is an immediate way to relax, socialize, and go after that buzz, which alleviates anxiety, eases their social awkwardness, and makes it easier to connect and make friends.

Yes, addiction and alcoholism run in families. Yes, your teen may be predisposed to addiction. This is different than how much your behaviors impact your teen's choices. Again, many teens who are raised with parents who do not drink at all may end up drinking. Contrast that with teens who witness their parents often drunk who choose to keep entirely away from alcohol. And, in between those opposites are all the other types of drinking a family may partake in: cocktail hour, watching sports, holidays, parties, socializing, or once or twice a year. It does not matter what *you* do as much as it matters when and how often your son *chooses* to try alcohol. This could

---

8 "Underage Drinking", National Institute of Health, accessed April 30th, 2019, https://pubs. niaaa.nih.gov/publications/underagedrinking/underagefact.htm

be in your home, but most likely it will be outside of your home. We cannot keep our kids locked up in their rooms. They live away from us for a large part of their day. Blaming yourself will not help your teen. Taking action will.

## YOU ARE NOT ALONE

When you discover your teen is drinking you may feel embarrassed and that you have somehow failed as a parent. You may want to hide this issue from family and friends, anticipating that you will be blamed, or they might feel sympathy for you that your teen is making such "terrible" choices. I am here to remind you, that many parents catch their teens drinking and then keep it a secret, fearing the same judgments or that their teen will get kicked off a sports team or out of school. Or many minimize their teen's drinking, putting it in the "kids will be kids" box and ignoring it as if it were not a problem. I have worked with many adults who use this line of thinking. However, I also, work with their teens in many situations and teens will hide, underreport, and/or minimize the frequency of their use or adamantly lie about it to avoid consequences.

The risks involved with drinking are very real and based on statistics. Ignoring your teen's drinking and being in denial will only increase the chances your teen could get hurt from drinking. You are not alone; you are not to blame; you are in the company of many parents of teens who are facing the same situation. What is important is that you address the issue, which will help your teen avoid the risks associated with drinking. Take action instead of ignoring (even though ignoring the situation can feel like the easiest path; avoiding conflict and anger from your teen). Taking action will be the most helpful thing you can do for your teen.

Adding rum to the cake is a serious issue that must be addressed; not ignored, tolerated, or minimized. Navigating this territory with your teen can leave you with a severe emotional hangover; it can be exhausting to worry about your teen. Be vigilant and aware when it comes to this ingredient. Your teen has plenty of time as an adult to add rum to his cake. You are the one in charge; do all you can and know that you can't control your teen's every moment. Be proactive, reactive, or anywhere in between when it comes to addressing the use of alcohol with your teen. This is serious business and could be fatal or a lifelong battle of addiction.

## AND, THERE IS GOOD NEWS!

The good news is that most teens experiment with drinking and safely navigate their teen years without severe consequences. Many drink when visiting friends but then want to sleep over, avoiding drinking and driving. Today's teens are very aware that getting in a car with someone who has been drinking is dangerous. While your teen may drink too much, end up vomiting, and have a nasty hangover, thankfully, it wasn't to the degree of having to be hospitalized for alcohol poisoning. Most teens who drink in middle school, high school, college, the military, and their adult lives survive, and either drink responsibly as they age or stop drinking altogether. That is good news. The bad news is, as a parent, you just cannot predict the future. However, you can take action that is helpful instead of turning your back and minimizing the risks of drinking.

My professional advice is to send clear, consistent messages to your teen that underage drinking will not be tolerated. Then take action, be vigilant, avoid minimizing with thoughts such as: "at least he isn't into drugs," "I drank as a teen, don't they all?", "Just part of growing up." Instead, get help for your teen if you know they are drinking. Access your school's drug and alcohol counselor (if they have one), an AA group, a drug and alcohol agency who can properly evaluate your teen's relationship to alcohol and recommend a treatment plan, such as outpatient (attending meetings and classes at the agency) or inpatient (living at a treatment center for 20-30 days, typically). These resources help you and your teen realize the risks involved, and you can learn about chemical dependency. All of this keeps you firmly planted in reality, not in denial.

Doing *something* will serve your teen far more than doing *nothing*. I trust that you have used every good ingredient possible to raise your child. However, rum can get added to the recipe, as ingredients come from many sources outside of your family. This is not your fault; don't blame yourself. But DO intervene. It takes courage, consistency, and unconditional love to reach and support your teen (no matter their push back, which can be quite fierce). I know it's tough to face this head on, but I promise you it will serve your teen far better than ignoring the situation.

# BROWNIES

## MARIJUANA AND DRUG USE

Unfortunately, all too often many parents become familiar with one of the most common cakes of all—brownies! Magic brownies that is, with marijuana as the main ingredient.

Parents make counseling appointments when their teen is showing a lack of interest in school, grades are plummeting, and they are worried about his new peer group. They tell me they just don't know what is wrong with their son, but they know he is just not performing to his normal level. During the intake, I ask if they think he is smoking marijuana, using drugs, or drinking? Often parents will not be aware that their son is using one or all of these substances. When they bring their teen in to see me so I can assess what is going on with him, I will often find that, indeed, their son is smoking pot, sometimes daily or even as frequently as starting his day with it and staying stoned the entire day. Some teens will readily admit they use other drugs, and nine times out of 10, the teen will assure me that none of his drug use is a problem.

Often parents do not know the signs until their teen is impacted via school performance or attitude and behavior problems, which is when I find them seeking professional support. Many of the parents I work with minimize marijuana, putting it in the alcohol category of, "Well, I mean, at least he isn't into hard drugs." I strive during my counseling sessions to help parents change that belief system. There are too many teens I have seen who become very dependent on cannabis and lose motivation. Many I have worked with have gotten kicked out of school for either possession or being high. Most schools have a zero tolerance policy for drug use, so teens will find themselves suspended or expelled. Just like with alcohol, I share with parents and the teen accurate information about the detrimental effects of using marijuana and other drugs. I do not join them in minimizing drug use because using these substances can negatively impact their teen's success at school, sports, work, home life, and even with friends.

Parents, I know that the last thing you want is for your teen to go down this path. But once you have found out, there are many things you can do to curtail his use. Educating, monitoring, following drug and alcohol professionals' advice, and staying vigilant, all can help your teen know you are treating this seriously, and are very concerned about how this will impact his health, wellbeing and success.

## TAKING A CLOSER LOOK (HELPING YOU STAY OUT OF DENIAL)

Every year that teens are in school, their resistance to trying drugs and alcohol decreases. Therefore, between eighth and tenth grade, the number of children in a teen's school who are smoking pot more than doubles.[9] By the time teens are juniors or seniors in high school, many have tried drugs or alcohol. Marijuana is especially tricky territory for one main reason: it is readily available at school and parties, and the urban myth is that this is a safe drug. Most likely, your teen will have the mindset that marijuana is no big deal. Rarely do you find a teen who will say, "I know weed is harmful,

---

9 Buddy, T, Very Well Mind, "At What Age to Children Start Smoking Pot?" accessed April 30th, 2019, http://alcoholism.about.com/cs/pot/f/mjp_faq04.htm.

and I would never touch it," though he might say this about crystal meth, crack, or heroin. However, marijuana can be just as threatening to his overall health, motivation, and performance in these developmental years. The physical effect of smoking marijuana is not as life-threatening as cocaine or amphetamines, opiates, crack, alcohol, or crystal meth. However, when your teen starts smoking marijuana, several wheels are put into motion.

First, the narcotic effect is very soothing. Kids have stress during their teen years: school, fitting in socially, family, relationships, coming to terms with all their body changes (acne, height, weight, body type), and clothing style, where they fit in and belong. Once the soothing high of THC washes over them, it is a pretty easy and effective way to feel relaxed, with no problems, that it's all good. And, to share a pan of brownies with friends or strangers where everyone is calm, relaxed, and feeling good is a powerfully connective experience. Typically, teens high on THC do not find baseball bats and go hunting to smack someone over the head, rape, destroy, bully, jump off bridges, or do other risky behaviors, as they might do, unfortunately, with alcohol. Marijuana does not produce this type of high. Back in the 1960's when using marijuana began to be more mainstream, the message was to *make love, not war, peace man*, and *chill out*. Currently, many states have now legalized marijuana; therefore, adults can purchase not only medical marijuana, but dispensaries sell many varieties, depending on the desired effect.

**Today's marijuana is more potent than in the 1960s and 1970s. The average potency of pot has more than tripled in the past two decades, according to testing done for the federal government. This change in potency has occurred at the same time that many states legalized pot, and many other states are considering making it legal for medical or recreational use. When researchers looked at the potency of THC in a study in Colorado in 2015, there was as much as 30 percent THC; in comparison, the levels 30 years**

ago were generally below 10 percent. And, smoking marijuana with these high doses of THC may involve a higher risk of adverse health effects, such as psychosis or panic attacks[10]. Teens are getting brownies with extra delicious ingredients thrown in, creating powerful euphoric highs. Who can resist?'

One of the major problems with marijuana is that teens have easy access to it and even their parents may be enjoying the taste of magic brownies: some use for medical reasons, some use recreationally, and some use habitually. Teens can be at a friend's home where the parents share their weed, or they can just take a walk outside and smoke it, smoke while driving or eat it in cookies, candy, and other edibles. Many teens see this as a harmless drug and will defend its healing properties and safety. They will vehemently deny that it is addictive or even habit forming, saying they know they can stop anytime, but merely want to keep using.

Once teens discover brownies, they risk wanting a magic brownie every day. Why not? Who doesn't like a delightful morsel of chocolate with an extra buzz every day? It can become an inviting escape on a boring or stressful day. But, contrary to what teens will lament, teens can, in a very short amount of time, develop a dependency on cannabis. (Research is not in on whether we are dealing with an addictive drug, but cannabis does create dependency.)[11]

---

10  Agata Blaszczak-Boxe, "Potent Pot: Marijuana is Stronger Now that it was 20 Years Ago," Live Science, accessed April 30th, 2019, https://www.livescience.com/53644-marijuana-is-stronger-now-than-20-years-ago.html.

11  Norman S. Miller, "Marijuana Addictive Disorders: DSM-5 Substance-Related Disorders," Journal of Addiction and Research and Therapy, accessed April 30th, 2019, https://www.omicsonline.org/open-access/marijuana-addictive-disorders-and-dsm5-substancerelated-disorders-2155-6105-S11-013.php?aid=84734.

Teens may start experimenting and then end up using marijuana daily. However, as they continue, they gain tolerance, and the high they once felt is not so high anymore. Now life without it causes them to feel down, irritable, and out of sorts. Now life does seem more difficult without it.

This narcotic exposes your teen to a drug dealer. At times a dealer or friend will offer him a new high: pills, ecstasy, cocaine, oxycodone, and, more alarmingly heroin, has made a comeback, resulting in a national epidemic.[12] If your teen is enjoying getting high, why not bump it up a notch and try a new high? The chances are good that for every teen and adult with an addiction problem, marijuana was their first drug (other than alcohol).

Because so many parents feel marijuana is not that big of a deal in comparison to other drugs, their teen can get a jump-start on the path to dependency and addiction. Parents may minimize the impact of marijuana on their teen's life, sometimes chalking it up to a normal adolescent stage. However, marijuana can be one of the most threatening drugs of all. Here's why:

**THE RISKS**

- It begins his journey to managing his stress with a drug.
- It easily can become a daily or weekly habit.
- The initial high turns into using it to not feel bad when not using it.
- Motivation begins to wane, your teen can begin to lose interest in school, sports, activities, and achievement, and your teen can start hanging with other kids who feel the same way.
- Grades often drop, and his path to success in high school can be interrupted and stalled. When his grades drop, this will stay

---

12 "Understanding the Epidemic," Centers for Disease Control and Prevention, accessed April 30th, https://www.cdc.gov/drugoverdose/epidemic/index.html.

permanent on his transcript. This can keep your son from college, good jobs, or interest in his normal activities.

- You can be angry and frustrated with your teen's lack of caring and motivation, creating much more conflict at home.
- Your teen can now get more interested in the next high. Wherever he is getting his brownies, the next tempting morsel is only a text away.
- The Fred Hutchinson Cancer Research Center found that being a marijuana smoker at the time of diagnosis was associated with a 70 percent increased risk of testicular cancer. The risk was particularly elevated (about twice that of those who never smoked marijuana) for those who used marijuana at least weekly or who had long-term exposure to the substance beginning in adolescence.[13]
- Marijuana is expensive, and many teens turn into adults with lifelong dependency and use.
- Marijuana dampens the spirit, the pep, the zest for life, especially if used daily. It can zap the enthusiasm and drive of young people and delay, if not stop, their path to adult success.
- Caught with drugs at school can get your teen suspended for as many as thirty days. Caught another time, they can be permanently expelled from the school district.
- The legal consequences for the loss of time and money, stress, and hassle for your son getting busted for marijuana is extensive. Plus, he will need a drug and alcohol assessment and need to follow treatment recommendations. This means sometimes getting your teen to outpatient treatment groups two to five times a week or admitting them to an inpatient facility. Parents can pay $10,000 to $25,000 (or more) per month for treatment, insurance will often pay but, unfortunately, not everyone has this type of coverage.

---

13 "Marijuana use linked to increased risk of testicular cancer," Fred Hutch, accessed April 30th, 2019, https://www.fredhutch.org/en/news/releases/2009/02/marijuana.html.

It is so easily accessible and socially acceptable that continuing the use of this powerful narcotic can be a piece of cake. If you shop around a bit, you can find yourself a magic brownie almost anywhere.

## SO NOW WHAT DO YOU DO?

Some parents argue that they smoked marijuana as a teen, continue to smoke, and do not see it as a big deal. They are productive, work, raise their family, and are successful contributing citizens and have their brownies and eat them, too (similar to how many adults use alcohol). While this may be true for many, when it comes to your underage teen, advocating for the use of marijuana is not a good idea. I have run into situations with teens where he is busted for marijuana at school and ends up with his family in the principal's office. He witnesses this performance from his parents: "We are just shocked that our son would have anything to do with marijuana; this must be a mistake." All the while, the teen knows his parents use marijuana themselves. This deception is a mixed message, and teens are BS detectors. They lose respect for their parents' authority and judgment. When parents model that using a drug is OK (as long as you hide it and lie about it), their child can become very angry and upset that his parents are hypocritical. Teens will tell me "My parents put on quite the innocent display for the principal when I got caught with pot. Acting like they are so shocked so the principal would think they were such good parents. Pisses me off!"

Parents, when it comes to marijuana, stay out of denial and resist minimizing the risks of this narcotic. If you find out your teen is using, you need to talk to him, keep a lookout for paraphernalia, pipes, papers, vapor pens, images on his notebooks (numbers such as 420, drawing marijuana leaves, saying, "Oh Mom, it's not marijuana; it's the Canadian flag)" or smell it on him or in his car. Insist on urine analysis (UAs) that are random, not scheduled. Random means giving the UA without advance warning, as he may know many ways to dilute his urine or substitute it with someone else's.

You can have UA's at doctors' offices or drug and alcohol facilities or order kits online. Insist that your son have a drug and alcohol evaluation. Follow through on treatment recommendations. Have a zero tolerance attitude toward his love for brownies.

Until his UAs are clean, you might take away his car, his phone, or limit phone use to only your number (many drug connections are made from his phone) you can begin to give him back his privileges, continuing to still monitor UAs, along with an occasional room, backpack, and car search for any paraphernalia.

> A caution on the UAs: your teen is smarter than you are when it comes to beating the system because he gives this more thought than you do. While you are occupied with paying the bills and raising him, he has no bills or dependents, so he has more time to calculate how to get his needs met.
>
> "My parents always drug test me the first Tuesday of the month. I start smoking again on Wednesday, then start cleaning up the last week or so before the next test."

Some teens get UAs in outpatient treatment. Once again, this is not always so random. Perhaps, the first meeting of the month the group is tested. Then, of course, after a couple of clean UAs, parents are relieved that their teens are on the right path. Teens count on you to lose interest in your previous vigilance; consequently, they go under the radar and start again. So, maintain random UAs. Insist that he sign a release of information at the doctor's office so that you also get his results. You can insist on all of this, especially when you are legally responsible for him and are paying for his phone, transporting him to his friends, buying him a car, paying his insurance, and often giving him money. You are in charge. Moreover, many teens feel relief when their parents are vigilant. It is a good excuse to tell his fellow weed lovers, "I can't smoke for a while; my parents took away my car and are watching me like a hawk."

Your job is to protect and teach your teen how to live successfully in this world. It is up to you to take action and do all you can to steer the course of your teen's life away from any drugs he can access. It is always possible that you can do anything and everything and still not be successful. Parents can lose their kids to the world of drugs and addiction. At some point, parents are forced to concede that they have tried everything, and yet, their teen continues to use. This is a huge heartbreak for parents. Teens can fail classes, skip school, get fired from jobs, develop withdrawn attitudes, and can end up running away to use, or get arrested and involved in the legal system. This is not what parents thought they signed up for. When a teen is drug-seeking, it is a huge problem for parents and, unfortunately, can be a serious lifelong problem for their child.

However, insisting on treatment, Narcotics Anonymous meetings, and a no-use policy in your family does introduce your teen to these resources and a clear, consistent attitude that drugs will not be tolerated. Attending meetings and groups early in life can set the groundwork for his adult life; he will not seem so intimidated to access these resources later in life if accessed in his youth. Once your teen is eighteen, your influence decreases dramatically. You cannot do much of anything about his choices. You can cut off college tuition or other financial support. If you bought him a car you could take it away, stop paying for his phone or even have him move out. However, you cannot get him to stop using. Introducing him to treatment, meetings, and drug and alcohol counselors when he is still living under your roof will at least give him the message that help is out there and accessible.

**Brownies are tempting and delicious treats. Magic brownies add a powerfully euphoric ingredient, so why go back to regular brownies when you have tasted those magic ones? Hence, it is the beginning of a possible lifelong dependence on seeking the magic with not only brownies but, also with many other drugs.**

**Magic brownies look so much like the regular brownies, innocent and harmless. However, it is the magic, the high, the strong narcotic effect of these tasty morsels that can make any other regular cake seem uninteresting and mundane. And, if life begins to look like that, then your teen will pursue an appetite for a diet of magic, as life will not seem quite as special without it.**

## IS THIS MY FAULT?

It is only natural that, as a parent, you are going to want to blame yourself when you find out your teen was or is smoking pot and/or using other drugs. But remember, your teen is in contact with the world beyond your door for a large part of his day. And even if you were smoking pot around your teen for most of his life, this still does not mean your teen will choose to do the same. I have worked with many a teen who tell me that their parents and grandparents regularly smoke pot, but they do not want anything to do with it and find it annoying that their parents use. And, of course, some do use because their parents modeled this behavior. As a parent, you have to decide what behaviors you will or will not engage in around your teen. Teens can be introduced to marijuana at a sleepover, at school, at a cousin's home, at church camp, from a sibling, from a best friend, from a boyfriend or girlfriend, or on vacation, and the possible circumstances where a teen can decide to smoke pot are endless.

I worked with a teen whose parents smoked marijuana daily and encouraged her to join them. She described holidays as a day her parents were always stoned. She wanted nothing to do with pot; she was angry and resentful for her parents' habitual use and how it interfered with their relationship. So whether you do use substances or you do not use around your teen, she may choose to emulate you or do the opposite.

Feeling guilt and shame will not help you deal with this situation. What will help is addressing the issue directly with your teen and then getting professional help, being consistent with your monitoring until you know your teen is clean. And even after all of your attention to this problem, she may defy you no matter what you do. Again, teens can get hooked and habitually use no matter what you say or do. But, as a parent, your positive influence is taking action.

## ITS NOT ALL BAD NEWS

Many teens who try marijuana in their middle or high school years don't like the high. In my experience, it seems that the boys I work with take to drugs much more so than girls, but, of course, it doesn't matter what gender you are, use and dependency affect both. But, again, many girls I have worked with tell me they don't like the high, or it causes them too much anxiety. Some have said they have panic attacks. Boys report the same, but not as often. Teens may experiment but lose interest or just dislike the high. Most teens go on to lead healthy productive lives, with or without marijuana or other drugs they may have tried in the risk-taking teen years.

What did you try in high school? Your friends? Your partner? What is your relationship and your friends' relationship with those substances now? I would bet that most people you know are functioning very well in their lives, and I would also bet, that some are not and have a serious problem. While your teen is more susceptible to addiction the younger he uses drugs and alcohol, or is predisposed via genetics, many teens grow up to be responsible and productive adults.

As the parent of your teen, you can educate, monitor, seek professional help, follow through on the advice you get, and be consistent with your messages to your teen. Send the consistent message that using marijuana, drugs, and alcohol underage is not allowed in your home, your teen is to stay clean while under your roof, privileges can be taken away (phone, driving, social freedom), and as their parent, you will be vigilant. You may not stop your teen from having a lifelong problem with drugs or alcohol, but at least you will know you did everything you could to keep your teen healthy and substance-free.

# 7

## DEVIL'S FOOD CAKE

### LEGAL TROUBLE

"Hello, Ms. Garcia, this is security from Target, and we have your daughter, Maria, with us. She has been caught shoplifting. Could you come to the store as soon as possible?"

"Hello, Mr. Lee, this is the principal of your son's school. We have your son in our office. We found a pipe in his backpack. We need to have you come in for a conference."

"Hello, Mrs. Taylor, this is Officer Smith calling. We have your daughter in the back of the patrol car and need to have you come to the station."

Yes, your precious angel is up to some devilish activities. Shocked and humiliated, you pick your teen up from the place she has gotten into trouble.

**The obvious questions are these:**

**"What were you thinking? What has gotten into you?" And you may be met with one of these:**

**"I don't know! I wasn't the one who stole that!"**

**"That is not my pipe."**

**"We were just messing around; we didn't know we were going to get arrested for this!"**

**"The cops are just out to get me."**

**You may get a sobbing teen: "I don't know why I did that; I have never done anything like this before!"**

Your little cupcake may have morphed into a Devil's Food Cake! It can start with attitude; it can begin with behavior, or, which is often the case; it can start with both. It is normal to have an irritable or withdrawn teen with a bad attitude on your hands; after all, teens are not always the most pleasant people to have around. However, it is quite another challenge (and a heartbreaking one, indeed) to have thrown in all the usual ingredients to bake up that tasty cake, which are love, care, protection, and guidance, and then to find out that when you take your cake out of the oven, it has grown a couple of horns.

## SO NOW WHAT DO YOU DO?

When you get calls like these, they are a brutal wake-up call that your teen is headed down a slippery slope. Unfortunately, because it is often human nature to minimize something one does not want to get caught doing, it might be wise to multiply by five the number of times your teen has done something that you have found out about for the first time. Of course, this is not always the case. However, I suggest you use this formula to stay out of denial and be aware. Even though you, as her parent, are finding out about her behavior for the first time, this may not be the first time at all for your daughter. Therefore, you need to take action. Shoplifting, drug or alcohol possession, trespassing, fighting, and so on will come with legal consequences, perhaps mandated counseling, community service, educational classes, or even time spent in a detention facility. But as a parent, you should not only give your daughter consequences but explore the possibility that a deeper hidden issue is impacting your teen.

Having your teen see a counselor can help your teen talk out what she may now be acting out. When your teen can express herself honestly about her stress, pain or concerns, this can often prevent her from acting out her feelings and emotions by choosing negative behaviors. Perhaps, some changes are going on in the family: extra stress, separation, divorce, financial stresses, alcoholism, or problems with other siblings. Perhaps, if school is especially stressful, your teen may be struggling in classes or trying to find friends or fit into a social group. Your daughter may be hanging out with teens who are already little Devil Cakes. Your teen's need to belong can impact her good judgment. Plus, a person will often act differently in a group than individually; peer pressure can be very influential. Either way, these behaviors are a wake-up call for you to take action, get to the root of the problem, and address the issue. This is not a time to minimize, justify, or explain away the behavior. And more supervision is needed until you trust that your teen is back on the right path.

Teach your children that making good choices will serve them. If she sees the value to do well in school, is educated on the risks and dangers of alcohol and drug abuse, perhaps she will choose to hang out with a peer group that shares the same values and beliefs your family has taught her. Then you will have a much easier time raising your teen. Hopefully, your teen will monitor her behavior, without your motivation and consequences.

If, on the other hand, you provide too much extrinsic control, she may be dependent on your guidance and rules, and, therefore, she may choose behaviors to avoid punishment. Or she may merely sneak around to hide her behaviors from you. If you instead guide your teen to accept responsibility for her choices, tell the truth and be accountable, and accept the natural and logical consequences of her actions, her choices may shift to being more intrinsically motivated.

## WHAT HAPPENS IF SHE GOES TO DETENTION?

If your teen continues her devilish activities, you may end up dealing with legal troubles. If she is arrested for assault, stealing, breaking and entering, drug or alcohol issues, destruction of property, bullying, and threatening, and so on, she will enter the juvenile justice system. This is another form of extrinsic motivation when your teen fails to regulate her own behavior. You will face a world of fear and pain as you see your teen judged, sentenced, and ordered to spend time in a juvenile detention center.

In "juvy," your teen will have a room she may share with another teen, be subjected to an early lukewarm brief shower, be served a tasteless breakfast, and then may be involved in groups, exercise, and school on site. If your teen decides to act out and not cooperate, she can find herself in a padded safe room, isolated from anyone else. Unfortunately, she may be exposed to 'new and improved' ways to make Devil's Food Cake from more experienced 'cooks' who may then join her circle of friends after she is released.

When your teen is finally released, she will have a new companion, her probation officer. This is not necessarily a negative thing. By now your parental authority is challenged to the max; a probation officer is more intimidating and can keep a nice thumb on her behaviors. A few years of court-mandated counseling, drug and alcohol treatment, and detention can wake up your teen.

# I FEEL LIKE THIS IS MY FAULT! I MUST BE A TERRIBLE PARENT!

The most loving parents with the most exceptional parenting skills can still end up baking a Devil's Food Cake. Again, whatever ingredients you add does not guarantee that your cake will turn out perfectly. Cakes can fall, this can be a reflection of the environment, peer group pressure, society, and your teen's own unique DNA.

Your teen is exposed more than any other generation in history to outside influences. The Internet introduces her to worlds you may not even know she found online. Also, the mobility of driving, hanging out with friends, and time at school exposes her to many temptations, experiences, and opportunities.

> You cannot follow her around and monitor her behavior 24-7, plus that is not good parenting. Good parenting is providing a stable home environment, modeling healthy behaviors yourself, being open to listening, setting boundaries, and giving appropriate consequences. Protect her when you can, and then gradually let go and hope she keeps herself safe.

# THERE IS GOOD NEWS!

Our justice system recognizes that teens can make choices that have serious legal consequences. Therefore, our juvenile courts believe that rehabilitation and redirection outweigh having a teen start their adult life with a felony record. Most records are expunged when a teen is eighteen (not all, but most, depending on the seriousness of the crime). Many teens who have made very poor decisions end up with this being part of their past. Counselors often say, "teens act out what they cannot talk out." If your teen has a rough adolescent life, perhaps from home or school or both, or hangs out with a peer group who shoplifts, sells or uses drugs, or steals a car for a joy ride, she can find herself making poor choices. Due to the peer pressure and her need to belong, she may join her friends and get involved in making negative choices that she may not have made on her own. Some teens are "scared straight" when they get caught; others may keep up the bad choices and face more negative consequences. Again, we cannot predict teen behavior. Growing up, having a more developed brain, and the school of hard knocks can motivate a person to make better choices than they did in their teen years.

A bit more maturity can lead your teen down a new path as your daughter becomes an adult at eighteen. Possibly faced with adult incarceration and with the fact that her parents cannot rescue her from the law as an adult, your teen may, in fact, settle down and may choose to be a Spice Cake, instead of a Devil's Food Cake—not an Angel, not a Devil, but just a bit on the spicy side.

# SECRET
# INGREDIENTS

# HAVING YOUR CAKE AND NOT EATING IT TOO

## EATING DISORDERS

Tia was a bright, attractive, and accomplished junior in high school. She sought out counseling when she realized she was struggling to get out of bed almost every morning. Her usual sense of excitement for life seemed to have vanished. During our first session, she shared that she thought she might be depressed and expressed an ongoing sense of apathy.

"I don't get it. I think everything is okay. I don't know why I feel this way."

"When you say everything is okay, can you let me know what you mean?"

"Like, I get straight As, I work part-time at the shelter, and I really like it, I'm in all the advanced placement classes I wanted to be in, and I play soccer and volleyball, and stuff with my family is okay."

"So, what makes you think you might be depressed?"

"I don't know; I feel sad and sort of fidgety all the time, like I get nervous a lot. I'm worried. Yesterday I started to panic. What if my grades slip? What if I don't do well on midterms?"

I asked if she was struggling with school, and she said that she found school to be pretty easy. To better understand the full picture of her life, I asked about her relationship with her parents. She said it was good and that her parents worked hard and were busy, and that they were proud of her and all she was accomplishing. I asked her about her eating habits. She said it was okay, normal – no changes. I asked if she had been to a doctor. She said yes that she had recently had a good checkup. I asked if she was using drugs or alcohol to help her cope. She was clear that drugs weren't the issue. I probed further to see if she was having problems with her friends at school or work. She explained that she was lucky to have found some very supportive, loyal friends who would always stick by her side.

For the first three sessions, we discussed her symptoms and brainstormed options. What might help her to feel less stressed out, less anxious, less depressed? We discussed curtailing some of her activities, but she said that she liked staying active and would not want to quit anything she was doing. We discussed going on anti-anxiety medications, but she said she didn't want to try them.

While at first, I was perplexed, I soon noticed that whenever we broached the subject of what she may be eating that could impact her moods or energy level, she became more anxious and upset. Finally, after I revisited the idea of anti-anxiety meds, she opened up.

"I think that the reason I don't want to go on meds is that they might make me gain weight."

"Is weight something that you think about a lot?"

"Not really."

"Can you tell me a little about your eating habits? Like, what do you usually have for breakfast?"

"Well, in the mornings I usually have a few bites of an apple and maybe like, half of an oatmeal bar."

"And what about lunch?"

"I don't like to eat lunch. It makes me feel bloated. But I do drink a lot of water."

"Okay, what about dinner?"

"I try to only eat a few bites. I move the food around on my plate, so it looks like I've eaten more."

"Do your parents ever comment on your not eating dinner?"

"Well, they think I've eaten a big lunch, then I tell them I ate a big snack after school or had an early dinner at a friend's house."

"Do you ever feel light-headed or weak?" Tia paused, then nodded yes. She then shared that she felt that maybe she did have a small problem because no matter how little dinner she ate, she always felt bad about it like she had overeaten. She said she would go into her room after dinner and sometimes she would take laxatives or try to make herself throw up. And there it was. What was clear to both of us in that critical session was that Tia had an eating disorder. Tia was anorexic and bulimic.

While Tia was able to recognize that there might be a "small problem," she was unaware of how much real danger she was in physically. I spent the next few sessions educating her on the risks of her under-eating and purging. I shared with her that she could get very sick if she kept on this path, she could be hospitalized, and she could eventually die if she didn't start making some real changes.

Treating Tia was not simple or easy. She resisted the idea that she was in danger. But slowly, she did make moves toward health. She agreed to work with a medical doctor so she could be monitored physically. She agreed to go on anti-anxiety meds to help her overanxious behaviors. As trust grew between us, she opened up about what was underneath the eating disorder. Tia had low self-esteem and was a perfectionist. Even though she was high-achieving, a steady worker, a good athlete, and a loyal friend, she didn't feel good about herself. She often felt unattractive, too stressed, or just not good enough. She set the bar high for herself with school, her appearance, work and her own character and standards; striving to be a good girl and accomplish everything well. And, just when she was close to achieving her high standards she would raise the bar again, never feeling she was ever good enough.

At one point, Tia's parents came in for a family session. Her mother Sarah was distraught at having missed all the signs of her daughter's disorder. Tia admitted to her mom that she would purposely purchase and wear baggy clothing and that she worked hard to make sure her mom thought she was eating well. In tears, Sarah said, "I just thought, she was getting such good grades, and her boss loves her, her teachers love her, she's just the best kid. I mean I could tell something was strange at dinner time, but I wasn't sure how to even bring it up. I didn't want to cause a problem. I guess I was in denial."

We talked about how easy it can be to miss the signs and, in turn, to be happy about all of her daughter's accomplishments. I let her know that it was common for teens to hide their eating disorders and that many parents miss the signs. We worked on Sarah not beating herself up and getting on board now to help her daughter.

Treating Tia was not swift or easy. It was a solid combination of medical oversight, talk therapy, meds, and ongoing education. We often had to review the health risks of having anorexia. We had to work on Tia reporting what she was eating accurately, as she was so used to lying or underreporting. She worked with her doctor to monitor her weight to avoid being hospitalized. We delved into her self-esteem and began to build a stronger sense of self, session by session. Over time, she accepted the gravity of her situation. As our treatment ended and we parted ways, Tia knew she was facing a serious, lifelong issue that would require ongoing monitoring of her body, mind, and spirit.

Since she was so high-achieving in so many areas of her life and generally a pleasant teen to have in her family, it was easy for her parents to miss this and only focus on all the positive outcomes they were seeing. Eating disorders are very hidden, and often parents have denial about their teen's eating disorders. It is scary to think about and difficult to have a conversation, especially with a teen who looks like she is doing so well.

## THIS IS MORE SERIOUS THAN YOU MAY WANT TO THINK

Your teen is smart, makes great choices, does well in school, has an active social life, but something seems off. Your daughter rarely eats with you, seems to be watching her weight a bit too obsessively, and you worry she may have an eating disorder. At dinner, she has excuses for not eating with you.

"You know, I just ate, and I am full. Can I save it for later?" "It looks good, but I am just not that hungry." Getting this type of response, avoiding joining the rest of you at regular meal times, may be an indication that your teen has an eating disorder. Of course, there are other behaviors to look for, but if you start to see a pattern during mealtime, you may want to look a little closer.

From the beginning of your daughter's life, you have prepared meals that she would eat, enjoy, and often ask for more. But then she hits adolescence, and gradually you notice that she is avoiding meals. You start to suspect that maybe your teen is deliberately not eating. Eating disorders in teens can go under the radar fairly easily. Teens are masters at hiding their anorexia (starving themselves in response to a distorted body image) and bulimia (bingeing and purging to try to avoid weight gain). Remember, teenagers are in the most self-conscious period of their lives. The last thing your teen wants is for you or her friends to find out she has a problem.

The hiding of an eating disorder is very typical. Your teen doesn't want you to know, her friends to know, anyone to know. It is very easy for her to hide her eating disorder. Risking being found out means not only embarrassment and shame, but the bigger risk is that she will have to eat or be watched so closely she cannot purge after eating. This means to her: "I am going to get fat; if I get fat, I will not be popular or liked, and I will hate myself." This secret your teen is keeping empowers her; she is in control of her body, and the more weight she loses, the better she feels. It is not surprising that parents are often oblivious to their child's eating disorder. Until a parent notices her very thin body or hears the teen vomiting after eating, he or she is not aware of the problem.

When teens come into counseling, they are often very resistant to letting me know they have an eating disorder. They will complain about many social issues, relationship issues, family issues, but openly sharing with me that they avoid eating, are terrified of gaining a pound, or purge after meals is not something they readily want to discuss. If they do discuss it, they are not motivated to change. They are very attached to the secret they are keeping and the control they get from starving themselves or getting rid of their food when they do eat.

## THE RISKS

**WARNING SIGNS OF BULIMIA INCLUDE:**

- **Extreme preoccupation about being overweight**
- **Strict dieting followed by high-calorie eating binges**
- **Overeating when distressed**
- **Feeling out of control**
- **Disappearing after a meal**
- **Depressed moods**
- **Alcohol or drug abuse**
- **Frequent use of laxatives or diuretics**
- **Excessive exercising**
- **Irregular menstrual cycles[14]**

---

14 "Understanding Eating Disorders in Teens," WebMD, accessed April 30th, 2019, https://www.webmd.com/mental-health/eating-disorders/understanding-eating-disorders-teens#1

## ANOREXIA NERVOSA WARNING SIGNS

People with anorexia nervosa typically weigh themselves repeatedly, portion food carefully, and eat small quantities of a narrow variety of foods. Anxiety, depression, or difficulty concentrating may also accompany these warning signs:

- Relentless pursuit of thinness
- Unwillingness to maintain a healthy weight
- Extremely disturbed eating behavior
- Distortion of body image
- Intense fear of gaining weight
- Over-exercise
- Misuse of diuretics, diet pills, or laxatives[15]

Symptoms of eating disorders may also include the following:

- A distorted body image
- Skipping most meals
- Unusual eating habits (such as eating thousands of calories at one meal or skipping meals)
- Frequent weighing
- Extreme weight change
- Insomnia
- Constipation
- Skin rash or dry skin
- Dental cavities
- Erosion of tooth enamel
- Loss of hair or nail quality
- Hyperactivity and high interest in exercise

---

15 "Anorexia Nervosa," The Emily Program, accessed April 30th, 2019, https://emilyprogram.com/what-we-treat/anorexia-nervosa/?

## TAKING A CLOSER LOOK AT BULIMIA

If she has bulimia, she may hide her disorder, feeling guilty and embarrassed that anyone would find out she is purging (regularly engaging in self-induced vomiting or abuse of laxatives, diuretics, or enemas) after a period of bingeing. Often, teens with bulimia will not be as thin as teens with anorexia. Some teens with bulimia can be overweight, so this disorder is often difficult to detect. You may catch her vomiting. This could open an honest conversation, or she may thoroughly convince you that everything is OK. You may want to believe her, as this problem is stressful and worrisome for a parent. You may feel helpless, not knowing how even to begin to help your daughter. Teens with an eating disorder need professional help. Having an eating disorder can be a serious health problem.

Purging can ruin the stomach, the esophagus lining, and teeth from the acid reflux or vomiting, and in severe cases, can prevent keeping food down at all as the body can malfunction, ending up with involuntarily vomiting after every meal.

## TAKING A CLOSER LOOK AT ANOREXIA

A teen with anorexia often prides herself on her control. She can feel dizzy from a lack of blood sugar and calories, and she often enjoys this rush. She can feel immense fear and guilt if she does indulge in food and then is terrified that she may have gained a pound. Consequently, she will work even harder to not eat the next day, exercise excessively, use laxatives, or starve herself even more.

Anorexia can deprive your daughter of needed nutrients. Having little body fat can interrupt and stop her menstrual cycles, she can lose hair, and tragically, because of the lack of electrolytes and other complications, anorexia can be fatal. Anorexia is a serious disorder that must be addressed and treated.

Once you discover that your daughter has one or a combination of these disorders, you must seek professional help. Have her see a medical doctor along with a counselor who specializes in eating disorders. Depending on her height and other factors, if your teen's weight falls below a certain threshold, she may need to be hospitalized or admitted to a specialized residential program.

## STRATEGIES YOUR TEEN MAY BE USING

Your teen will make up all kinds of excuses for why she does not want to eat when everyone else does. She may ditch her friends for lunch at school and prefer to hang out in the library, in a classroom, or her car, making excuses she is still full from breakfast or already had lunch. She may secretly throw her lunch out, and may, at the very most, nibble on a few bites of an apple slice, already feeling anxious that she may have overeaten.

At dinner with the family, she may play with her food, spreading her food around her plate, or state she is not hungry. When questioned about what she has eaten, she might lie and report that she's had a typical breakfast and lunch, merely telling you what she knows you want to hear.

## THIS IS SO SCARY, WHAT NOW?

If you find out that your daughter is refusing food or bingeing then purging, it's time to take action. These are serious health issues that, if left unchecked, can be detrimental to her health and, in some cases, fatal. Open up a conversation with your daughter about her eating habits and noticeable weight loss, and let her know that you have some serious concerns. If she heads to the bathroom during or right after her meal, follow her to the bathroom to see if you hear her vomiting. If she is looking too thin (though teens will often wear baggier clothes to cover their weight loss), then bring her into the doctor to have her weighed. It can be life-threatening if her weight drops too low.

Often when parents find out that indeed their teen is refusing food or turning her nose up at meals, they may hover to be sure she is eating. However, a teen with an eating disorder does not want you to try to get her to eat. She is attached to her image of being thin; therefore, when you attempt to monitor her eating or make a big deal of how little she is eating, it only builds resentment and stress for her. Teens with eating disorders strongly identify themselves with a thin body image and can have a distorted body image, seeing themselves as fat when they are underweight. If she is not always striving to be thin, or if she loses control and binges, she can fear rejection, disapproval, and complete loss of control.

Do not be critical, harsh, or send out "eat, eat" messages to your teen. Do not share her eating disorder with your family or friends unless your daughter wants you to. It is embarrassing to your teen, and she can be adamant that no one should find out, let alone everyone. Do be loving, supportive, and seek the guidance of professional help. Not only will you sleep better when your teen joins the family when it is mealtime, but you will rest reassured when she chooses to eat her slice of cake for dessert.

## IS THIS MY FAULT? DID I DO SOMETHING WRONG?

As a parent, you have not caused your child to have an eating disorder. There is not just one factor that contributes to the disorder. Experts are still researching what causes these disorders, from a combination of social messaging, media (such as all those ads and magazine covers displaying thin women) genetics; family influence; and physiological and psychological problems. Researchers are looking at the impact of playing sports such as gymnastics, swimming, dance, track, or running, where being lean is encouraged. In one study, researchers linked anorexia with an obsession with perfectionism

-- concern over mistakes, high personal standards, and parental expectations and criticism.[16]

While it would be far more helpful for your teen if you did not make any comments about her body weight, even if your intentions are purely health-related, a teen whose body is changing throughout puberty can interpret any comments as criticism or as a goal she needs to achieve to be loved and accepted. Your comments will not cause her to have an eating disorder, but your voice in her head will influence her confidence and self-esteem.

> It is far better to compliment your teen no matter her body size or to let her know that you love her without any comments about how she is developing or if she has put on weight. Your daughter gets plenty of messages from her life outside of your home. It is essential that your words veer far away from her body and instead address her "inside self;" her attitude, character, heart, and mind.

This does not mean ignoring the issue when you suspect a disorder, but it does mean letting your child know that not eating can negatively impact her health and having her see a doctor can help her with her nutritional needs, keeping her on the right path and not having the scales plummet to a life-threatening weight.

## THERE IS GOOD NEWS!

There is hope. Teens can overcome these disorders with professional help and the support you give her. The causes of anorexia and bulimia are still not en-

---

16 "Perfectionism Linked to Eating Disorders, " Web MD, accessed April 30th, 2019, https://www.webmd.com/mental-health/eating-disorders/news/20030205/perfectionism-linked-to-eating-disorders.

tirely known by the medical or psychiatric community, and treatments vary. Start with your family physician to discuss treatment for your daughter, then look for a counselor who specializes in eating disorders and have your teen get professional support. There are a variety of treatment centers and programs, some in the US, some in other countries. The internet or your health care provider can provide you with options. The best hope for navigating eating disorders is bringing it into the light, not keeping it a secret that your teen is hiding from you. Talk to your teen with love and concern, focusing on the health ramifications, not her size. Many teens grow out of their eating disorders in their adult lives, and sadly some struggle their entire lives. Again, there is no predicting the outcome. However, with your support and action, your teen will be in a much better situation to overcome these disorders.

# DARK CHOCOLATE CAKE

## MENTAL HEALTH ISSUES

In high school, Josh was interested in film, video, and media arts. He came to see me at the urging of his parents, who felt he was depressed and not coping very well with his parents' divorce. He presented as shy and guarded. But as our sessions continued, he began to trust me more and shared with me what he was thinking and feeling. Yes, his parents' divorce was difficult, along with adjusting to his dad's girlfriend as the result of an affair. But both being movie buffs, he and his dad did enjoy going to movies and films together. What Josh's parents did not know was how dark Josh's thoughts were.

"Well, this is hard to share, because you will think I am crazy, but I get very violent "bloody" images in my head. And when I am at the pool (he is a lifeguard), I would get compulsive thoughts at times of seeing myself drowning students." He claimed he was not suicidal or homicidal because he knew the difference between his thoughts and actions. But his mind was full of violent imagery. He had even fantasized about planting bombs underneath his parents' staircase. What is most disturbing about Josh's mental health is that his parents had no clue. How could they, unless he shared the innermost parts of his mind, which they would be shocked to hear about?

Josh's thoughts were hidden and dark, and he knew better than to share them with friends or other adults. Thankfully, he shared them with me so that we could have open and honest conversations about them. He did agree to go on an anti-de-pressant/anti-anxiety medication, which seemed to decrease his violent images and compulsive thoughts and boost his social life as he spent less time being isolated.

Ten years later, Josh is a very successful and optimistic young man, with a bachelor's degree in film, a lovely fiancé, and he seems to be enjoying life past his dark teen years. Mental health issues are often hidden, and a teen's mind can go to many places, which most parents have no idea about. Thankfully, Josh was not suicidal or homicidal, both of which are a result of depression and impulsiveness and are a lethal combination for many teens and a devastating heartbreak and shock for parents.

## THE MOST COMMON MENTAL HEALTH ISSUES WITH TEENS (WHOM I HAVE TREATED IN MY PRACTICE)

When parents call me, worried about their teen, it often has to do with the mental health issues that this chapter discusses. While I am not covering these issues in great detail, and your teen should only be diagnosed by a healthcare professional for accuracy, I did want to provide an overview since you may have chosen this book because you are seeing some of these symptoms with your teen.

More than ever, teens are dealing with issues of anxiety and depression. I have my own theories about this (that would need to be an entire other book), and there is a lot of current research on reasons for the increase. I do think that my theory and other research agrees that the increase of isolation is due to social media, texting, and teens being more vulnerable to bullying and attack, which contributes to their angst. Teens already feel vulnerable enough when they step foot on school grounds; are their clothes just right, their hair, their look? And now, teens can be photographed and video-recorded anywhere and anytime, which can then be shared with thousands of people without their permission. Can you imagine if this was your experience in high school when you were at a party, social event, sleepover, or engaging in any social activity? Their privacy is invaded, which can contribute to feeling more anxious and depressed.

Teens with mental health issues can often be confused with teens who have normal angst and adolescent irritability. It can be easy for parents to overlook issues that need to be treated by a mental health counselor, psychologist, psychiatrist, or family doctor.

**Teens can be diagnosed with:**

- adjustment disorder,
- depression,
- bipolar disorder,
- anxiety disorder,
- posttraumatic stress disorder (PTSD),
- obsessive compulsive disorder (OCD),
- attention deficit disorder or attention deficit hyperactivity disorder (ADD or ADHD)

to name a few of the more common diagnoses. These mental health disorders are treatable, and with medication and therapy, they will often improve. If your teen has these symptoms, it is best to seek the guidance of a professional for an accurate diagnosis and treatment.

## DEPRESSION

Depression can be quite serious. When things seem darker to your son, you may see symptoms of withdrawal. He may want to spend too much time to himself. You observe anger and irritability, and you are concerned that your teen seems unhappy. Your teen could feel alone, detached, sad, and overwhelmed with the everyday things in life. However, too scared to talk about his feelings and thoughts, he keeps them to himself. You might discover your son expressing his dark side with pictures or writing, sometimes violent or questioning in nature, and exploring the purpose of life, lost love, or more directly, losing the will to live, that life is just too hard, or that life takes too much energy to cope.

Depression also can manifest as loss of interest in once normal activities. Your son may be unmotivated to finish schoolwork, go to class, or participate in sports or other activities. Signs of depression are revealed when teens are just not functioning as optimally as they could. This is not a good time to try to talk your teen out of his mood with pep talk comments such as: "pull yourself up by your bootstraps" or "look at the bright side." These comments may make you feel better but won't help your son. He may feel you are minimizing his feelings and that can make him feel ashamed or angry which could result in him withdrawing even more, often feeling misunderstood.

## WHAT CAN I DO TO HELP MY TEEN?

Depression is a treatable mental health disorder. Your teen may have a genetic predisposition to depression (you can often find this in the extended family) and adolescence has now exacerbated the symptoms. Or, your teen may be suffering from situational depression. This can be grief from trauma or loss (illness or death of a loved one, family stressors or divorce, the breakup of a relationship, social rejection from good friends or his clique at school, or bullying). Either way, your teen can often feel relief with professional counseling and antidepressants.

There are other possible reasons for his depressive symptoms, so have your teen get a medical checkup. There could be a lack of nutrients, hormones, thyroid or iron deficiency, a hidden eating disorder, drug use, or other physiological problems, so it is best to rule out any other possible health factors. If your teen is prescribed antidepressants, you must keep a close eye on him. This means observing that he is taking his medication and seems to come out of his slump, which could take two to four weeks. Also, it is the best practice to have him see a counselor every week for at least the first two to three months that he is taking this medicine. In some rare cases, the antidepressants can do the reverse and make the depression worse. If your teen does seem to get worse, he needs to be taken off the dosage and then prescribed a different type of medicine that will work as it should. A teen on antidepressants can do quite well, helping him get back to a more familiar self, and as his parent, you will be relieved to know he is feeling better, doing better, and coping better with his life.

## NEVER UNDERESTIMATE THE WORST POSSIBILITY

In the worst case scenario teens attempt suicide. Teens tend to have impulsive behaviors. For example, if he has a relationship break up, and if that collides with other stressors, your son can feel overwhelmed and not able to cope, resulting in a suicide attempt. Teens can also overdose on antidepressants, acetaminophen or any pills they can find. Boys seem to choose a more violent method such as using guns or hanging themselves, while girls seem to either take pills or cut their wrists. Because depression can be so hidden from parents' awareness or even the teen's friends, the suicide of the teen is often unexpected and always tragic. Grieving family and friends look back to see what signs they had missed, searching for any clues that this nightmare could have been avoided. Again, teens can be impulsive. Suicidal adults can live with thoughts of suicide for years and never follow through with an attempt. Or if they do commit suicide, it is often less impulsive than a teen and more planned out. A teen may impulsively attempt suicide as a solution. If there is a secret that he is keeping, or if he feels unloved, outcast, bullied, socially harassed, or his relationship breaks up, he can attempt suicide, not giving much thought to other solutions to help him cope with his pain.

> Any talk of suicide or an attempt is a cry for help, and parents, you must pay attention. During my career as a therapist, I have heard parents say things such as, "I think he is being dramatic" or "He just wants attention," and, in so doing, they minimize their son's Dark Chocolate symptoms. Parents, because of the often-impulsive nature of teens, always err on the side of caution and take seriously any threat of suicide and talk with him, or have him talk to a counselor, trusted adult friend, suicide hotline, doctor, or clergy. Keep pills, knives, and guns locked up. While you cannot predict a suicide attempt, since teens are often secretive and impulsive, keeping weapons and medicines locked up can make it much more difficult to follow through on his impulsive thoughts.

## TRAUMA

Post-Traumatic Stress Disorder (PTSD) is an ongoing or delayed response to severe trauma. This can manifest as depression, anxiety, irrational fears, or phobias, nightmares, flashbacks, or disturbing mental images about the trauma.

There are often hidden causes of PTSD that you may not know about. This could be the sexual or physical abuse of your teen that has not been disclosed, and, this abuse could have been one incident in his childhood or adolescence or can be an ongoing abuse he has kept hidden. The death of a parent, friend, or sibling, a trauma suffered (house fire, car accident, life-threatening or long-term disease or illness), witnessing stressful events or learning about an unexpected or violent death or injury to a family member or close friend,[17] these can all create a post-traumatic response. Teens need a safe place to talk about what they are feeling and thinking and a caring adult who can validate and value what they are going through. Once again having a professionally trained counselor onboard to educate and treat the symptoms of PTSD with your teen will provide good support.

Therapies strongly recommended for treating PTSD are Prolonged Exposure (PE), Cognitive Processing Therapy (CPT) and trauma-focused Cognitive Behavioral Therapy (CBT). When researching a good therapist for your teen, it is entirely acceptable to query the therapist about their credentials and experience when offering PTSD treatment. [18]

## ANXIETY AND PHOBIAS

Anxiety disorders and phobias can manifest as your teen resisting attending school or avoiding social activities and crowds. She may have a panic attack, or she may not be able to stop obsessive or compulsive thoughts. If you are worried that your teen gets too stressed and witness her crying, having angry outbursts, or generally emotionally falling apart, she may indeed be suffering from anxiety. Today's teen is often overbooked with demands of school, sports, activities, and a busy family life. All of these burdens can contribute to your daughter feeling anxious or experiencing a panic attack, either of which frightens her and you. There is medicine that effectively treats anxiety disorders, and she can be taught how to manage her stress with the help of a professional.

OCD (Obsessive Compulsive Disorder) can manifest with symptoms

---

17 Shirin Hasan, MD, "Post-traumatic stress disorder, " Teens Health from Nemours, accessed April 30th, 2019, https://kidshealth.org/en/teens/ptsd.html.
18 Laura E. Watkins,' Kelsey R. Sprang, and Barbara O. Rothbaum, "Treating PTSD: A Review of Evidence-Based Psychotherapy Interventions," accessed April 30th, 2019, https://www.ncbi.nlm.nih.gov/pmc/articles/PMC6224348/.

such as rigidity to keep her room perfect, having to keep things just right (clothing, backpacks), sticking to a rigid routine and feeling distressed if it changes, or being adamant about hand washing, germs, or engaging in other repetitive behaviors. Her thoughts keep repeating as if her thoughts were circling in a roundabout in her head and she can never escape. OCD can also be treated very successfully with medication and therapy to calm down her obsessive and compulsive thinking. Taking your teen to a professional will educate and support her and also help support the family.

Bipolar disorder can be a more challenging diagnosis, as teens often have mood swings, and it is difficult to sort through what is normal adolescent behavior and what are bipolar symptoms. This disorder is typically diagnosed with severe mood swings and impulsive choices by your teen. He may seem overly energetic, talk fast, and be "manic," which can also result in angry outbursts and violence. After the manic mood, he can then drop into a state of depression, low energy, and apathy. These moods can rapidly cycle or cycle at a slower pace. Because of normal adolescence, with its ups and downs and hormone fluctuations (premenstrual syndrome (PMS) can look a lot like depression), and mood swings can be the norm throughout these turbulent adolescent years. It is best to get an accurate diagnosis and treatment before jumping to the conclusion that your teen has this disorder; however, it is a valid diagnosis and does respond well to treatment.

Getting a correct diagnosis is essential before treating depression or bipolar disorder, as the medicines used to treat each diagnosis are different in each case. Work with your teen's counselor and health-care provider to get the right medication to give your teen the help he needs. Some things cannot be treated with a positive attitude and require medical intervention.

Attention deficit disorders (ADD or ADHD with hyperactivity) can reveal themselves in early adolescence. Your teen can start slipping with his school performance in middle school when his schedule moves from one primary teacher to several teachers and classes per day. Juggling several classes and several teachers can influence the success of a student with ADD. These teens have a difficult time focusing, staying organized, or following through on school assignments. To sit all day in a classroom and focus can be agony for a teen with ADD/ADHD. You may find your son beginning to fail classes, get into trouble in class, and start underperforming. You know he is smart and capable, but he has a difficult time applying himself.

ADD and ADHD can be treated with medicine and behavioral management with very positive results. It can make a world of difference for teens. Some parents do not want to put their teens on prescription medicine; however, teens who are treated medically for ADD or ADHD often have more success in school. Sometimes the change in them is like night and day. They can focus, follow through, sit still, and all in all, perform better. Since their education is so vital to their future choices and successes in life, medically treating these disorders can maximize your teen's progress.

## ADJUSTMENT DISORDERS

Adjustment disorders are situations in your teen's life when there is change that results in an increase in stress: moving to a new school, going through a divorce in the family, losing a family member or friend, adjusting to the breakup of a relationship, adjusting to a parent's divorce, or living with stepparents. Any situation that throws a teen off of his normal daily routine, where he has to adjust and adapt, adds stress to his mind and body. Often, with some extra support and time (perhaps six months or so), he can start to feel grounded again and feel much more capable of coping with his life.

A teen's initial adjustment disorder can evolve into depression and/or anxiety if it goes on too long without relief. With adjustment disorder, most people stabilize within six months to a year if life becomes routine again. However, if this lingers more than six months be aware your teen can become depressed and more anxious and may need to be treated for these symptoms. There are many types of adjustment disorders, some with anxiety, depression or mixed feelings. Many people seeking counseling support are experiencing an adjustment disorder. Time can usually help, but extra support can assist during this troubling time.

## PERSONALITY DISORDERS

Personality disorders are usually not treatable with medicine but can be managed with boundary setting, awareness, and knowledge. The borderline personality disorder is one of the more common diagnoses made in the teen years. Your teen can show symptoms of depression, have difficulty regulating her emotions, end up cutting herself, feel lost or empty inside, or have difficulty maintaining social relationships. Teens can be manipulative and have mood swings and can also go on binges *without* having a borderline personality disorder. Any diagnosis in teen years should be made with caution and with a professional. It can be challenging to sort through normal teen mood swings and behaviors during these years in contrast to a valid mental health diagnosis.

Parents may seek counseling for their teen when recognizing that something is not right. Counselors are skilled at working with personality disorders and can help your teen gain a new perspective, increase self-worth, learn to manage her emotions, and build better social relationships. There is a lot of conflicting research on how one develops a personality disorder, and normal adolescent behaviors can mimic a personality disorder. The counselor can help you understand your teen's symptoms and the course of treatment needed.

## WHAT CAN YOU DO TO HELP?

Having a teen with a personality disorder can be very confusing. However, if you are worried about your teen and how he seems to be behaving, I would have him see a counselor; those who work with teens are very skilled in diagnosing mental health disorders and personality disorders. If you do not have access to a counselor, I would suggest reading articles or books on these issues so that you are informed about the symptoms and possible treatments. Your doctor can medically treat mental health issues. The personality disorders at times respond to medicine; however, consistent boundary setting is usually one of the best methods, (as some personality disorders present with highly manipulative behaviors), helping your teen regulate emotional responses and even mindfulness training can help.  Again, if you have access to counselors, it is best to have one on board.

One important piece of information when choosing a counselor is that you might need to "shop" for one who is a good fit for your teen. Otherwise, you may end up stopping counseling explaining; "We took her to a counselor a couple of times, but she didn't like the counselor, so we stopped." Getting a counselor with whom your teen clicks is essential! Shopping for a counselor is perfectly OK. The best resource is asking the school guidance counselors or your health care provider if they can recommend a licensed counselor or psychologist whom they have heard works well with teens. Or, perhaps, other parents you know have a teen seeing a counselor whom they like. Getting a personal recommendation is your best bet. Not all counselors work with teens or work well with teens. Ask many questions when finding a counselor regarding his or her training and background. You want your teen to connect and feel comfortable.

Your teen may prefer to work with either a male or female. The counselors who are less clinical and more warm and friendly may be the best bet for your teen. (Condescending or parenting-type counselors are not a good fit for teens.) Teens are a bit apprehensive about talking to an adult in the first place. If your teen does not click with his counselor, he will not trust him, and then may not open up.

Your teen may be surprised and pleased that his confidentiality is protected under the law. Once he finds out the counselor will not tell on him, give him consequences, or suspend him from counseling, he will learn to open up and trust him. (Every client is told the exceptions to professional confidentiality, such as sexual or physical child abuse, neglect, suicidal or homicidal suspicions, which must be reported to the appropriate agency for intervention beyond the counseling office.)

Your teen may share things with his counselor you had no idea were going on; drug or alcohol abuse, incest, stress, and anxiety about his family life, sexual identity issues, social pressures, eating disorders, or suicidal thoughts. If your son has a good relationship with his counselor, you will find peace of mind from that extra support during these tough years. Find a licensed counselor or psychologist he likes and then follow through on treatment recommendations.

If you do not have insurance that pays for counseling, check with your local community mental health center or social services to see if there are less costly resources available. There are now counselors who work online or through Skype, FaceTime, or secured websites (tele-counseling). Your Dark Chocolate Cake needs that extra support to help him cope with this difficult stage in his life.

## THE GOOD NEWS

All of these mental health diagnoses are treatable medically. It hasn't always been this way, but with new prescription drugs and counseling that effectively treat Depression, PTSD Anxiety, ADD/ADHD, OCD your teen can get relief, have a better quality of life, and in many cases, they can save your teen's life. Medical intervention combined with counseling is the best combination for success. While some parents worry about the drugs' side effects, and while it is true that any medicine has side effects, in my experience, teens respond very well to prescription drug treatment, and the side effects are so minimal that I, personally, rarely hear a negative comment about them from my clients.

The teen years are often very confusing for parents. Your teen can be surly, oppositional, moody, withdrawn at times, or most of the time. You might wonder what happened to the child you used to know. It can be frustrating to think your teen is depressed, especially after you have done everything you can to give your child a great life. You might take it personally; however, I am reminding you that your teen's behaviors, attitudes, and choices are not all about you. Many of the teens I have professionally counseled over the years, have been suicidal, anxious, lacking confidence and often feeling isolated, lacking a social life, and/or are angry with parents. I have also seen well-adjusted teens, popular, busy and high achieving, having angst, and many with depression, suicidal thoughts, and anxiety. Since I have had a career for over 30 years, I now hear from teen clients who are now adults, and they are leading normal adult lives: working, in relationships, raising kids, they have good friends, etc. No sign of those turbulent teen years is evident. The teen years are tough, but they end, and your teen grows up, learns new coping skills, and overcomes many of the struggles of those difficult years. While it is true that they can still be dealing with mental health issues, their ability to cope is more solid, and they are less self-absorbed. This, too, shall pass, but until it does, take these issues seriously and get professional help when you can.

# SPECIAL INGREDIENTS

# 10

## POUND CAKE

### OVERWEIGHT AND BULLIED

Emma's mom wanted her to see a counselor, as she felt Emma was depressed, avoiding school, and often irritable and angry. Emma presented with a smile on her face, a bit shy, and she was about seventy-five pounds overweight. Our sessions together revealed two main issues.

Emma was being teased and bullied at school due to her size. Comments were thrown at her on bus rides to and from school and during the day at school. She was left out of being chosen for PE activities and often shunned from conversations in the classroom. She was very aware of the petite, skinny girls in her classes who seemed to exude confidence and self-esteem. She was not invited to dances or had any dating experience. Emma had a couple of girlfriends at school but avoided social media and did not have much of a social life after school. Feeling excluded from peers was painful; Emma preferred to sleep in and avoid school. When she was irritable and angry toward her parents, it was because home was a place to let down and vent.

The second issue was her parents' messages to her. Their attempts to comfort her made things worse. They wanted to help her go on a diet with a nutritionist; they monitored her food intake with comments such as, "Emma, do you really need the bag of chips?" Her dad made it worse by commenting on her eating behaviors when ordering in restaurants, as he was embarrassed by her weight. Parents struggle with this very sensitive topic on how to support their teen. No parent wants their child to be bullied or left out due to not fitting the social norm, so naturally, parents will want to solve the problem so their teen fits in better and they can curtail their own pain and worries. However, making these intended to be helpful comments are only received as criticism, resulting in more shame. Emma is not alone when it comes to being harassed due to her appearance. High school and social media can be a daily hostile environment for students who do not fit the popular body type.

## FITTING IN AND HOW PAINFUL THAT CAN BE (FOR YOU AND YOUR TEEN)

If your teen is overweight or obese, she may be coping with low self-esteem issues because of her size. Teens today are heavier than ever--childhood obesity has more than doubled in children and quadrupled in adolescents in the past thirty years.

> **In the United States, the percentage of children and adolescents affected by obesity has more than tripled since the 1970s.[1] Data from 2015-2016 show that nearly 1 in 5 school age children and young people (6 to 19 years) in the United States has obesity.[19]**

---

19 "Childhood Obesity Facts, " Centers for Disease Control and Prevention, accessed April 30th, 2019, http://www.cdc.gov/healthyschools/obesity/facts.htm.

Becoming overweight or obese is affected by various genetic, behavioral, and environmental factors.[20] This is not a teen's fault, but a societal problem. The food available today is often densely caloric with empty, non-nutritional calories and easy to obtain with the number of fast food restaurants; packaged, ready-to-eat food; and processed convenience food. Teen drivers can now frequent any fast food restaurant. Teens often drink sugar-laden coffee drinks, eat unhealthy snacks, and drink sugary sodas. Many teens are busy running to practice, games, or other activities and often grab a quick and often high-calorie, low-nutritional snack.

Teens move less than any other generation to date, often sitting with their phones, computers, video games, or watching TV. The inactivity, the added hormones in food, the high-fructose corn syrup added to thousands of foods, the high fat of most fast food, and overly processed convenience foods all contribute to overweight teens. Teens may inherit genes that give them a more sluggish metabolism, so they may gain more weight than their fellow students even though they consume similar calories.

If you, as an adult, struggle with your weight and may feel at times embarrassed or socially conscious because of your size, imagine how your teen feels during the insecurities of adolescence? Teens are especially suspicious and sensitive to what others may be thinking about them. Teens think that they have an invisible audience around them who are paying attention to every single detail about them: their complexion, clothes, hair, and, of course, their bodies. We are a culture with media and advertising putting pressure on people to lose weight, be thin, and be in top physical shape in order to be healthy, sexy, happy and accepted.

---

20 "Childhood Obesity Facts, " Centers for Disease Control and Prevention, accessed April 30th, 2019, http://www.cdc.gov/healthyschools/obesity/facts.htm.

Overweight teens are often teased and bullied (usually by multiple people) throughout the day. Middle and high school students can be quite insensitive and cruel (thankfully, many teens are kind, thoughtful, and empathetic and would never think of being rude). Unfortunately, too many teens would rather tease, insult, put down, harass, and bully than be empathetic and respectful. These teens find overweight kids an easy target. Imagine the stress your teen is under when she, in this most sensitive time in her life, has to mingle with rude and mean-spirited teens five out of seven days a week at school or 24-7 via social media.

## WHAT CAN YOU DO TO HELP?

Unfortunately, approaching your teen regarding his or her size is tricky territory. It can come across as critical and only frustrates your daughter into feeling you are now bullying her by bringing her weight to her attention. Making comments such as "Are you sure you want that extra helping?", "Are you sure you should be eating that?", Or "You have got to exercise more! Want to come to the gym with me?" can result in making your daughter feel more self-conscious and resentful. As her parent, pointing out your daughter's body weight is painful and embarrassing. And, unfortunately, while your intentions may be honorable your attention and advice are not perceived as supportive and most likely will be received as criticism or an annoyance, and it can build resentment. Be careful not to make off-hand comments such as "I was watching a show the other day where teens had lost an amazing amount of weight; I thought you might want to check it out" or "Oh, by the way, I ran across a camp that helps teens lose weight and eat correctly." And, don't buy your teen a book on dieting and health and lay it on her bed.

There are some effective ways to reach your teen on this sensitive topic. Set the example without lecturing, hinting or making passive comments. Model making healthy food choices yourself and with what you cook. Teach portion control by encouraging smaller portions (so much food today is supersized).

Make your home a sanctuary of healthy food. Shop the outside of the grocery aisles where the "real" food is; fruits, veggies, lean meats, and whole-wheat breads. The inside aisles are full of overly processed foods. Parents are the nutritional gatekeepers of their homes.[21] You have a major impact on what your family eats by what you bring into your home. Have fruit out where kids can see it and grab it, or prepare healthy snacks for after school. If your home is devoid of chips, sugary cereals and sodas, candy, sweets, and high-fat foods, then at least you are avoiding the temptation of your teen coming home, looking in the cabinets, and grabbing that extra-sized bag of chips while plopping in front of the TV.

You cannot follow your teen around 24-7; they will find pizza, junk foods, and fast food restaurants more than you can ever monitor. If you make too big of a deal about what she is eating or her size, she will seek these foods out and overeat to spite you.

**Do not nag, criticize, point out, or express your opinion about what she orders or eats. Instead focus on all the positive things about your teen, the other ingredients that go into your unique and magnificent child.**

If your teen comes to you feeling miserable and wanting to get help, then, of course, this is your opportunity to get your daughter support. You can work with a registered dietician, your healthcare provider, and, perhaps, a personal trainer who can get your teen started on a fitness routine. If she wants articles or information on healthily losing weight, provide her with the

---

21 Ryan Wansink, *Mindless Eating, Why We Eat More Than We Think*, (New York: Bantam Dell, 2017, 162).

tools. However, do not make the mistake of working harder on her weight loss than she is! You might get so excited that she wants to make a change that you flood her with too many suggestions and resources. Instead, follow her lead at her pace.

## I FEEL LIKE THIS IS MY FAULT

Of course, you can feel that anything that affects your teen is your fault; you are a loving and caring parent. And while it is true that you are the one bringing the groceries into the home and can decide to bring healthier choices (instead of the dense-calorie, nutritionally void foods that are often loved by your teens), there are many other reasons why your teen may struggle with their weight. I have seen teens eat non-stop and never gain a pound, and then other kids start putting on weight during preadolescence. I have seen parents who are not overweight but have an overweight child, even when the home is full of healthy food. Much of the science and research is now focused on why some people gain weight more than others, even while consuming the same calories. And yes, you can stock your home with healthy choices, which can help your teen avoid that bag of potato chips, but you are still not to blame if they are gaining weight. Teens choose what they put in their mouths, and again, they are not always hanging out with you. They are in school, at friends' homes, driving, at sports events, camps, malls, etc. Kids hang out at many places outside of your home and are influenced by many food choices.

## WHAT MATTERS MOST

Your teen is well aware that she is not a size zero like many girls she may compare herself to every day at school. However, she has the same needs as anyone, no matter her size, and that is to be *loved, respected, valued,* and to feel like she *belongs* and is *capable* and *successful.* Affirm how smart, capable, and beautiful she is; no matter what her size is, assist her in finding trendy clothing and compliment her on all her qualities, without focusing on her weight. She has more than enough societal messages from the media, peers, and family about how thin is the only acceptable way to be! She has years ahead to find her way regarding her size, confidence, and self-acceptance and esteem.

As a teen, she is already self-conscious and anxious about her looks and how others may be judging her. Teens feel like a magnifying glass is on them at all times that exposes them to possible ridicule and bullying, especially at school, on social media, or at other sports and clubs they belong to. Home should be your teen's refuge; where she can count on feeling loved, supported, and accepted for who she is; a safe and secure place to be. If she feels she is your project or is put down by you or her siblings because of her size, she will feel shame at home and school. If you always remind her that you love her unconditionally and that you think she is perfect just the way she is, she will find refuge from the often painful world of measuring her value by her size. You have the most crucial role with how your teen values herself, so ignore any temptation to coach her regarding her weight, and instead be affirming, supportive, and always her biggest fan!

# 11

# RAINBOW LAYERED CAKE

## YOUR LGBTQIA TEEN

Marco moved from a more progressive city to a smaller suburban town. His parents wanted him to see a counselor as they felt he was having trouble adjusting to his new high school. Marco was a gay Latino teen moving into a predominantly white, conservative community. Marco was, in fact, having trouble adjusting to moving away from his friends and now trying to make new ones. Marco was out of the closet and openly gay in his previous school. He had the support and advocacy of his parents, who are very supportive and accepting. However, he had a tough time fitting in at the new school.

There were a few girls who immediately befriended him. He is friendly, intelligent, and witty. However, the majority of the male students would not accept him. He heard snide comments, was called names, and when walking down the halls of the high school, male students ("jocks" as he referred to them with their letterman jackets) would block him and elbow him as he tried to pass. This continued harassment

**was foreign to him for the most part because of his previous, positive school experience. He was frustrated, discouraged, and overwhelmed with the effort it took to go to school every day and put up with this harassment.**

**Marco's parents were heartbroken and were second-guessing their move. They had moved because both parents had better career opportunities, and they were taken aback that their son was being bullied since he had been so popular in his previous school. They advocated for his safety with the school staff and provided him a very loving home, but they felt helpless to protect him at school and in his social life. Even with the support of his loving parents, Marco was having an extra tough and stressful time attending high school.**

In the past ten years of my counseling practice, I have seen such improvement for LGBTQIA teens (Lesbian, Gay, Bisexual, Transgender, Queer/Questioning, Intersex, Asexual)[22] when it comes to acceptance. The teens I work with are usually out and open about their identity and have friends and fit in at school. Some report bullying and harassment, but this is so much less frequent than it was beyond ten years ago. I am so pleased, at least where I live in the greater Seattle area, that our society has become more open and supportive. We have a long way to go, but things do seem better, at least where I practice.

Parents can still struggle with their teen's sexual and gender identity and orientation, but most of that comes from fears based on how society will treat their teen, possibly rejecting or shaming them. I realize that in many parts of the country and our world, it is very difficult for teens who are LGBTQIA.

---

22 LGBTQIA Resource Center, UC Davis, accessed April 30th, 2019, https://lgbtqia. ucdavis.edu/.

They are harassed, bullied, rejected, shamed, and at times physically hurt or murdered. If you are an accepting and supportive parent, your teen is indeed fortunate.

Adolescence is a rough time for any teen; however, it can be especially rough on the teen who is LGBTQIA. When it comes to bullying, high school is the perfect place; it is the only place in a person's lifetime where you will find this many teens gathered under one roof, who often have low self-esteem, are insecure, and immature. If your teen is a boy who meets a girl, and that girl may or may not like him back, your teen is already struggling with matters of the heart and intense attraction. However, if your teen is a girl who likes a girl, or a boy who likes a boy, he or she can find adolescence a suppressing nightmare.

LGBTQIA teens may find themselves in very isolated and lonely situations. Being attracted to the same sex, these teens may need to keep their feelings to themselves to avoid being bullied. Coming out in high school takes courage and risk. The brave teens that do may be embraced by teens who are open and accepting. Unfortunately, it may be likely that they will be met with a heavy dose of teasing, bullying, and ongoing harassment. The homophobia of some straight and gay students can even be life-threatening to gay teens. (Yes, gay teens can also be homophobic: because there are so many negative stereotypes about gays, lesbians, and bisexuals in popular culture and religion, gays and lesbians often turn that into hatred for themselves, this is called internalized homophobia.) Internalized homophobia can be blatant, like the person who attempts to change their sexual orientation by Reparative Therapy or the young LGBTQIA person who attempts suicide because they would rather be dead than be gay.[23] And, boys are much more likely to be hurt physically; lesbians can be labeled with rude and stinging comments daily.

---

23 Kathy Belge, "What is Internalized Homophobia?" accessed April 30th, 2019, https://www.liveabout.com/what-is-internalized-homophobia-2171094.

## THE RISKS TO YOUR TEEN

Lesbian, gay, bisexual, and transgender teenagers are two or three times more likely to attempt suicide than other teens[24] If the families of the LGBTQIA youth do not accept them, they are eight times more likely to commit suicide than other teens. One-third of the suicide attempts that result in death are due to a crisis in sexual identity. LGBTQIA youth miss more than five times as much school as other students because of the bullying they receive at school. Twenty-eight percent of LGBTQIA youth stop going to school because of being bullied.[25]

**The National School Climate Survey conducted by GLSEN in 2011 reported the following statistics on bullying:**

- **Eighty-two percent of LGBTQIA youth had problems during the previous year with harassment about sexual orientation.**
- **Sixty-four percent felt unsafe at school due to sexual orientation.**
- **Forty-four percent felt unsafe at school due to gender identification.**
- **Thirty-two percent did not go to school for at least one day because of feeling unsafe.[26]**

Along with being harassed and bullied at school, teens may not have parents or extended family who will accept the fact they are LGBTQIA. For

---

24 stopbullying.gov, accessed April 30th, 2019

25 "LGBTQ," StopBullying.com, accessed April 30th, 2019, https://www.stopbullying.gov/at-risk/groups/lgbt/index.html.

26 "2017 National School Climate Survey," GLSEN, accessed April 30th, 2019, https://www.glsen.org/article/2017-national-school-climate-survey-1.

these teens, there is no safe refuge to be who they are. Your Rainbow Layered Cake may have an unbearably stressful time going through adolescence.

Some parents with a gay or lesbian teen would rather stay in denial and not address the issue that their teen is gay, lesbian, bisexual or transgender. And to compound the denial, parents may send endless messages to their lesbian daughter such as "Don't you think that boy is cute?", "Did Justin ask you to homecoming?", or "Why don't you wear more feminine clothing; you dress like a boy, for heaven's sake."

To their gay son, the messages may be: "You want to be in the school play? What, are you a sissy?", "How come you never ask a girl out?", "Who are you taking to the prom?", or "Stop acting like a girl, for heaven's sake; man up."

---

**If your teen has the courage to come out, the parent's response could be harsh:**

- "You think you are what? Oh, for heaven's sake!"
- "What is it with teens these days?"
- "Is this some popular new phase?"
- "This is just a stage; every teen goes through this to some extent."
- "What is the world coming to? Kids are so mixed up these days."
- "Don't tell your dad; he will flip!"

**Even if you are an accepting parent and are supportive of your teen, you may still give out messages of secrecy and shame: "It's OK that we know, but let's not tell your grandparents; they are from a different generation, and they may not understand," "Let's just keep this between us. We know you are gay, but you don't need to go around advertising it to everyone. Let's keep this in our family."**

If your teen is the lucky teen who has parents who listen, support, and provide any outside support for him (counseling, LGBTQIA support groups, books, and articles), he is fortunate indeed! However, if you are not one of those parents and are struggling with the suspicion or reality that your teen is gay or trans, you might consider getting professional help or educating yourself on what it means to be a parent of a gay or trans teen and future adult. There are several books, websites, and support groups that will provide information, answer those questions you have, and ease some of your anxiety and grief: "My daughter will not walk down the aisle with a handsome groom!", "What about grandchildren?", "What if someone hurts my son?", or "What about AIDS?"

> **Your town may have support groups for parents; a typical group may be called LGBTQIA for youth, where there will be plenty of company and support. PFLAG (Parents and Friends of Lesbians and Gays) is excellent support for parents. Knowledge is power, and this may very well be a time to seek extra help.**

## SCARY NEWS

The suicide rate for gay and trans teens is much higher than heterosexual teens during adolescence.[27] The rejection from his family, the hidden secret he alone knows, not being able to visualize a future for himself, and dreading how he will fit into society, along with bullying and harassment, can be too much in these fragile years. As a parent, you may not always know that your son is struggling with these issues; he may even be dating girls to hide his

---

27 "LGBT Youth," Centers for Disease Control and Prevention, accessed April 2019, http://www.cdc.gov/lgbthealth/youth.htm.

true feelings. Teens can be pros at fitting in, not wanting to draw attention to themselves to avoid rejection or harassment. It is possible that your son may be homophobic as well. Gay people are often in denial themselves or live in fear that they are different than their heterosexual friends. If your family holds any religious beliefs that homosexuality is wrong, it may be even more difficult for your teen to come to terms with his sexuality.

## TRANSGENDER TEENS

There are also situations where the teen is not gay but transgender. This is a person who has an inborn sense of and identifies with, a gender identity that differs from the one that corresponds to his or her anatomy. Transgender people who are born with male anatomy identify as female and those who are born with female anatomy identify as male. Some transgender teens know they are different from the time they are young. Others start sensing it around puberty or even later. When transgender teens become aware that they feel mismatched with their bodies, they may feel confused and emotionally conflicted.

If you are an open and accepting family, it is best to get professional support and education to understand your teen. In many cases, your son may, at some point, engage in the process of changing his physical body to match his gender identity, through surgery or taking hormones to match the female he is. Physically becoming the opposite gender can be a long, complicated, and expensive process. Not all transgender people decide to get surgery or hormones; some are more comfortable keeping their physical anatomy or by changing the way they dress. Some are not entirely sure what they want yet.

This situation is very tough for parents as well as the teen. For some parents, learning that their son identifies as a girl (or their daughter identifies as a boy) can be shocking. In the beginning, parents may feel a range of emotions, including disappointment and a sense of loss. Some parents, though, may have already suspected it and are not surprised.

## WHAT YOU CAN DO

Educating yourself on this topic and getting support will help your family navigate this territory more effectively. Many websites and organizations can educate you as a parent. Even when the news is unexpected or difficult to hear, it's important for parents to react with love and understanding. Experts say that even a slightly accepting attitude is helpful. Since gender identity is not a choice, trying to force a child to change his or her gender identity is not helpful and can lead to problems.

## THIS IS NOT ABOUT YOU

Parents want to search for answers when they are worried about their children. And if you are concerned that your teen may be struggling with gender or sexual identity, you may be looking to blame yourself. Was it some ingredient you added to the recipe while raising your child, or something that you did or did not do during your pregnancy? Was this something that had to do with how you raised your child? Or, perhaps, you blame yourself for not knowing sooner, for not paying attention to the fact your son wanted Barbie dolls, not cars and trucks when he was a child. Maybe you did not want to accept that your daughter preferred to dress in boyish style clothing, keep her hair short and want to play sports with all the boys.

You may be feeling all sorts of conflicting emotions. However, you are not to blame for your child being gay, lesbian, bisexual, transgender, questioning, intersex, or asexual. Biology is what it is; your child was born the way that he is. While some teens may choose to explore their sexuality during adolescence, questioning their attractions or preferences, an LGBTQIA teen does not choose their gender or sexual identity any more than a heterosexual person chooses his or hers. Teens (as well as adults) may experiment sexually and with expressing their gender identity, but most land on solid footing and learn who they are inside. As a parent, you cannot change who your child is; educating yourself, getting support, and loving your teen unconditionally is how you both will navigate this territory in the healthiest of ways.

## THE GOOD NEWS

The world is changing, in some places faster than in others, when it comes to embracing and supporting LGBTQIA people. Movies, television shows, social norms, laws and policies, politics, and celebrities have paved the way for people to come out and be who they are, and now gay marriage is legal in the United States. Make no mistake, there is still a long way to go. In many countries, death is still a punishment for LGBTQIA people, and many religions and belief systems condemn lesbian, gay, and transgender people. The US and the UK have initiated many laws and policies that support LGBTQIA people. This is progress, and our younger generation is much more accepting than many among the baby boomer and World War II generations.

The best news, though for your teen, is how you, as a parent, support your teen. When you are open and accepting and are side by side with your teen, learning together about who he or she is, the challenges he or she is facing, and finding resources for both of you, that will be the most invaluable gift you will give to your child. While you may feel scared for your teen, or even, perhaps, sad for yourself, you accept the fact of who your teen is, not who you thought they were or would always be. You are then far ahead of so many families that want to stay in denial or try to change their child into someone they are not. Love, acceptance, and support will be the best ingredients you can add to help your LGBTQIA teen thrive in adolescence and well into his adult life.

Rainbow Layered Cake has been around from the beginning of time. It can be quite colorful and festive. It has always had a place in our traditions, and it is not going anywhere. To embrace that the world offers a variety of cakes in many styles and flavors is to accept life for what it is: diverse, interesting, and with an endless variety of delicious ingredients!

# 12

# SPONGE CAKE

## PASSIVE BEHAVIORS

Isaac's parents insisted that he seek counseling as his grades were plummeting and he was failing two classes in his sophomore year. Both parents came in with Isaac and discussed their son's declining grades. Isaac did not talk very much and avoided eye contact. His parents clearly wanted me to "fix him." My sessions with Isaac revealed that he was feeling suppressed and stifled. His family was religious and very involved with their faith and church activities. Isaac began to resist participating in Sunday classes and the worship services. His parents were not pleased. He knew that they felt very strongly that it was their duty to raise him as they saw fit until he was eighteen and then he could make his own choices.

Isaac was respectful of his parents but was raised to accept and not challenge their authority. Isaac found some personal power in avoiding classwork and failing classes, as a passive-aggressive way to rebel, as outward rebellion in this family was completely unacceptable. He also pierced his ear on his own and started wearing all black clothing with sayings

**on his t-shirts to which they highly objected and about which they were furious. His parents were devastated, since the last things they wanted were school failure or any more piercings or rebellious clothing. They felt helpless that they could not motivate him to be more successful in school or wear more respectful clothing. Isaac's parents thought that they had added all the right ingredients to raise an upstanding young man; however, he certainly had other ideas.**

You may be raising a teen who does not seem to ever express an opinion, who keeps to himself and complies with what is asked of him. At times, when parents add too much authority to the mix, whether it is because they are strict or rigid or have strict, conservative, religious expectations, the cake that they are baking may turn out to be a Sponge Cake.

This teen sponges up everything in his environment without questioning, developing, or expressing his own opinions and feelings. In rare cases, he will outwardly rebel. He does not have many choices, because his parents have imposed most of his decisions from their (extrinsic) outward expectations. Their teen often reluctantly complies with the parents' demands to avoid argument and the possible consequences for going against their authority.

When there is simply no parental tolerance for questioning, curiosity, discussion, arguing, and making choices outside the family's beliefs and values the family can raise a teen who feels isolated and insulated from the "other world" they live in during the school day, as it is different from what they are taught at home.

Often, the families of these teens practice strict fundamentalist ethics. They may be Christian, Muslim, Mormon, Seventh Day Adventist, Jehovah's Witness, or another religion with a more conservative code of expected behaviors than other religions or spiritual paths. These teens often soak up their parents' religious teachings without question. Beliefs and values are taught by their family, not explored independently. Or, perhaps, there are no religious factors, but the style of parenting is authoritative, "my way or the highway," "kids should be seen and not heard." It is understood that the parents are in charge and challenging their authority will not get a teen anywhere other than possibly in trouble.

While the parent can find baking a Sponge Cake fairly easy, it can also result in a passive teen who ends up being a passive adult. Passive adults can struggle with asking for what they need and want in their relationships, sticking up for themselves, or they participate in behaviors below the radar to gain personal power (passive-aggressive, avoidant, forgetful, or any other strategy that seems innocent enough but negatively impacts those around them).

Being raised in a Sponge Cake family means the power comes from the top down. Being raised in other cake families means there is the natural struggle for power from the teen toward his parents' authority and the parents' attempts to keep control over their teen. When the power from the top is accepted, it can result in such compliance that all motivation is externally provided, weakening any internal motivation. Teens raised like this may go on as Sponge Cakes in their adult lives, still staying the course and living by their parents' rules, never fully discovering who they are, what they like, and speaking up for themselves.

Once away from home, away from his parent's authority, he simply delays the rebellious stages of adolescence. Since the external power is removed now, the young adult has to make choices on his own. He may begin experimenting with alcohol and drugs, thinking he has a lot of catching up to do compared to his friends who started this in high school. He may act out sexually or feel a loss of control. And, of course, this must stay very hidden. Along with leading this double life, he may feel guilty and ashamed. And he knows if his parents found out they would be extremely upset, which could result in rejection from his family.

This teen has no opportunity to build his internal drives, beliefs, values, or ability to say no to peer pressure since the family provides it all. Plus, guilt and shame are heavily internalized. Therefore, when he becomes an adult, he may struggle with the ability to make choices from an autonomous place. Instead, he attempts to please whom he is dating, his friends, and anyone else but himself. He can delay gratification or live in a world of denial, denying his own experience, feelings, and thoughts to do the right thing or please others. Since he desires to have some power and influence over his own life, this can result in passive and sometimes aggressive behaviors. When asked to do a task, he may "forget," or when asked to comply, he may not follow through. In relationships, he may never speak up, allowing himself instead to be bossed or ordered around, as this is how he was raised, and this is his norm. People in relationships with him can feel frustrated, as he is not direct but indirect, indecisive, and avoidant. This power imbalance in the relationship can result in his relationships being more parent to child (he as the child) than adult to adult.

**Raising Sponge Cakes may look a lot like raising Angel Food Cakes; however, there is a big difference. Sponge Cakes absorb the environment in which they are raised in as the parents carry all authority of decision-making and provide the beliefs and values about life. Angel Food Cakes have a more flexible environment, where the parents live by their beliefs and values, and, at the same time, encourage and empower their teen to explore and come to his or her own conclusions, creating an environment where the teen feels loved and accepted for the choices he or she makes. Moreover, Angel Food Cakes who do choose riskier behaviors know that their parents are there for them and that they are loved and guided and will not be rejected.**

## WHAT YOU CAN DO

If you recognize that your parenting style is authoritative, and you seem to be raising a great kid, note that underneath all that compliance may be a suppressed individual who may be stifling his voice and ability to problem-solve on his own. Instead, if you can encourage discussions and seek opinions, your teen will learn early on to speak up, express his thoughts and feelings, and will feel that you are respectfully listening. The upbringing your teen receives is powerful, and no matter what, your voice will be in his head throughout his lifetime. If you mix in a bit more flexibility while raising your son, you may end up, in the long run, with an autonomous adult who can make good choices for himself in all of life's situations. He could develop direct, instead of passive communication skills, and live the life he wants to live, often adopting many of the beliefs and values he was taught as a child, much to the delight of his parents.

After all, the will and spirit of a person is strong. The freedom to be who he wants to be and not whom his parents want him to be is most likely going to happen whether his parents like it or not. As you parent, consider less top-down authority (especially when the teen's age is between sixteen and nineteen) and more guidance and wisdom to assist him in transitioning to his adult life.

## THE GOOD NEWS

Teens raised in authoritarian or strict religious families are often given a foundation with good morals and guidelines for being a respectful teen and adult. Many teens who rebel against their parents' authority and religion end up accepting the fact that their parents thought they were doing what they were supposed to do according to their beliefs and values. As teens become adults, they can often forgive their parents for how they were raised (having felt suppressed, shame or guilt) realizing that their parents believed what they were doing was in their teen's best interest.

You have the right to parent as you wish, according to your beliefs and values. There is no recipe that guarantees success when parenting; there is too much evidence that many adults who are healthy and successful in life may have had turbulent and distressing childhoods. And some adults who were raised in loving and supportive authoritarian or permissive homes may lead unhealthy or unsuccessful lives. There are so many more influences on a person's choices in life than how they were raised. Do your best, make adjustments along the way as needed, and no matter what style of parenting you implement, you can always let your teen know how much you love and value them.

# 13

## NO-NAME CAKE

### INTROVERTED TEEN

Adam was a sophomore when his parents brought him in for counseling. They were worried about his grades and the impact of his relationship with his mom. His parents had been divorced since Adam was eight, but his mom was very codependent on the men in her life and gave more attention to her boyfriends than to parenting Adam. As a result, Adam lived with his dad and his stepmom when he started high school in ninth grade. Adam had a sharp wit and sense of humor but was resistant to counseling. He admitted he found it stressful to visit his mom, as he had no respect for her newest boyfriend. But, he also enjoyed his younger brother's company who lived with his mom, so he tried to make the best of his visits. His dad and stepmom owned a business together and were very busy, so he spent a lot of time at home alone.

Adam's issues were much more significant than coping with his parents' divorce and subsequent back and forth visitations. Adam had no friends. He had been in this school district since kindergarten and told me he had never had a friend; he had never been to someone else's home or had anyone over to his home. At school he rarely had anyone say hello to him or notice that he was there. In counseling, we explored what he could change socially, but as a junior, he felt like this was just the way it would always be. He did not cause trouble at school, his grades were mostly average but low in some classes, and he had no interest in alcohol or drugs.

He described coming home to an empty house and playing video games for entertainment. I worked with his parents to get him involved in any opportunity to find social connections and to make some friends, as he had given up trying. Adam stopped coming to counseling after about three months. His parents felt helpless about getting him more socially engaged. They were concerned about suicide (as was I), but Adam did not claim he had such thoughts.

There are many "Adams" in our schools who have few, if any, social connections or a group where they fit in; belonging and being accepted meet one of our most essential human needs, and whether by suicide or violent acts, this level of isolation is indeed a potentially dangerous situation. In fact, in Adam's senior year, it was discovered that he was planning to set the trash cans on fire in the school bathroom in an attempt to burn the school down.

You may find yourself a parent of a teen who does not fit into any of the other specialty cakes mentioned thus far in these chapters. You may find yourself wishing for a piece of a more "normal" cake at times. Perhaps, your teen is a quieter teen; a teen that seems to prefer to keep to himself, likes to be in his room, often on the computer or playing video games. He never makes any waves, likes school, gets good or decent grades, and he appears to have very little desire for a social life.

He rarely gives you any trouble, has no interest in drugs or alcohol, or is not all that interested in a relationship or attending sporting events or other school activities, such as dances or proms, or joining clubs or other social activities. He seems interested in a good game of chess and lots of computer and video games. He dresses more conservatively without much attention to style or trends.

> You may be raising a teen who could be referred to as a nerd, a geek, or more professionally, he may be diagnosed with Autism Spectrum Disorder.[28] All of these labels point to one thing for you as parents: you are raising a cake with No-Name, a cake that can be "invisible" to all the other teens and even adults.

Your quiet, introverted teen, with very few social skills, can be quite concerning to you as his parent. You fear that he may be a social outcast at school, ridiculed, lonely, and not fitting into a peer group. Moreover, when your son does socialize, it may be about topics that are either way over the heads of other teens or just not that interesting to the average person. Your teen may love to learn and may absorb information like a sponge. He may excel in specific subjects such as technology, history, computer science, math, and science.

At times your son seems surly or irritable; you may even experience some explosive episodes. However, more than anything else, your teen can seem, for the most part, emotionally detached. He is not a teen who shows many

---

28

feelings; in fact, it seems your son mostly lives in his mind, deep inside himself. You worry that he will never be like normal teens or adults. Also, you may worry about how he will adjust to his adult life, leaving behind the protection and love of the family nest

> You may find yourself envious of the other parents who chat about usual worries about their teens; their teen was caught attending a party (*I wish my teen would want to go to a party*). Or you may feel envious of your friends whose teens are out and about, finding that perfect outfit or attending school social events (*my teen has no interest in style or school dances*).

Teens who are diagnosed with ASD seem to be more prevalent in today's world.[29] These teens usually have a few friends to hang with, and are, for the most part, more comfortable at home. As they become young adults, they might attend college and focus on their studies and expand their social circle as they mature. Even if your teen is not diagnosed with ASD you may have a teen who is very shy and introverted.

Raising your quieter, introverted teen can be challenging, as many of these teens (even during childhood) can be very particular about sticking to routines, having strong likes and dislikes for specific foods, and an inability to be flexible with transitions. If your family plan changes unexpectedly, all hell can break loose with an explosion from your typically passive teen. Also, when having family or friends over, your teen may avoid eye contact and avoid being friendly or welcoming and instead may show an attitude of indifference, often embarrassing you in normal social situations.

---

29 "Autism Spectrum Disorder," National Institute of Mental Health, accessed April 30th, 2019, https://www.nimh.nih.gov/health/topics/autism-spectrum-disorders-asd/index.shtml.

It takes a tremendous amount of patience to raise a teen with No-Name. From birth throughout all of your child's life, you knew your child was different from other kids of his age, but you couldn't always put your finger on it. At times, he would not tolerate his other playmates, being rigid as things had to be his way, so consequently, friends would refuse to interact with him, leaving him socially isolated. Of course, this was often a heartbreak to you as his parent.

## WHAT CAN YOU DO?

If you are raising other specialty cakes in your family and have one No-Name Cake, you may worry more about this one: "How did our son turn out this way? Did I have a normal pregnancy? Was it something I did?" But more than that: "Will he have a normal social life? Will he find someone who loves him?"

You are not to blame any more than you get credit for your other teens who are extroverted and social. We are all born with DNA from our family tree and from conception we are evolving into our unique selves. Your children are already pre-wired for many of their personality traits. You can help, though, by how you respond and nurture your teen.

You are your teen's most important resource since he prefers to spend most of his time at home and not out socializing. This adds more burden to you than many parents who have teens who find any reason to be with friends, away from their home. You are the primary support system, which is stressful and a lot of responsibility for a parent. You may get very frustrated, and your patience can wear thin, while your worries and concerns about how your teen will ever fit into society continue to grow.

I recommend that you give yourself some grace and that you do not blame yourself when you get frustrated. It is a lot of responsibility and worry when your teen only wants to isolate and/or is constantly rejected by his peers. It can be a heartbreak for sure. You can support your teen by exposing him to as many outside interests and groups of people as you can. These could be martial arts classes, church groups, camps that pique his interest, guitar lessons, support groups that counselors can offer, one-on-one counseling for building social skills, limiting screen time, and encouraging other interests such as art, music, or playing board games with him.

Look into alternative school programs, STEM (Science, Technology, Engineering, and Mathematics) schools that may be a better fit than the mainstream high school. Your teen needs to find a place where he feels he belongs, and often the regular high school is not a good fit. Most school districts offer STEM programs or alternative learning.

Your older teen may be a good fit for Running Start programs, which allow him to take his Junior and Senior high school classes at the community college for both high school graduation requirements and college credits. There is less high school drama, and more maturity on a college campus and bullying would be less likely.

Many school districts offer technical schools within their high school programs. Teens can learn how to create video games, computer programming, coding, and many other interesting programs.

If your teen is in a smaller district without these alternative opportunities, it is very important that you find community resources outside of school to help your teen to feel a sense of value and belonging. Perhaps, having a job or volunteering at food banks or pet shelters, interacting with senior citizens, being involved with church groups such as Young Life. Getting your teen out of the house and socializing will build his confidence and teach him social skills. Baby steps may have to be taken to coax him out of the house and into new experiences, so start small, if needed, and even resort to bribing and rewarding to get him to agree to try new things.

## THE GOOD NEWS

As your teen matures and enters his adult life, many of the "nerdier" teens turn out to be very successful adults especially in the technology, engineering, or science industries (Bill Gates or Mark Zuckerberg, for instance). No-Name Cakes may be attracted to a more outgoing partner who keeps social ties active. When girls abandon their interest in the Devil's Food Cake boys, these No-Name Cakes can be quite a prize! Often rich with great character, stability, loyalty, and financially successful, they can be a considerable source of pride for the parents who once worried they would not fit into society. Also, while they may never be big communicators and are often shy or introverted, they often find themselves more comfortable in their adult skin than during those peer-driven teen years.

When you create a nest where your teen can be himself, feel emotionally safe, secure, and loved unconditionally, you have provided the very best environment for your child. Your home is his refuge during these very trying teen years. He will fare better in his adult life, away from the cliques and often insensitive and cruel comments of some teens in high school. He has a safe, supportive, and loving home and that is the very best a parent can provide.

# SURPRISE INGREDIENTS

# 14

## UPSIDE-DOWN CAKE

### COPING WITH DIVORCE

Leticia came to me her sophomore year, as her father felt she was depressed. She was missing school, her grades were down, and she was gaining weight and sleeping more. She was also cutting on herself, which was the final straw that prompted her father to get Leticia to counseling. Leticia's dad was worried about her home life with her mom. Describing her mother as hot-tempered and angry (she especially hated her ex and let her girls know), Dad was worried that Leticia was stressed from coping with her mom's moods. Her mom was against her going to counseling, so it was her dad who was motivated to get her help. Leticia presented as friendly, smiling, and engaged in our conversations. As our sessions progressed, it was clear that Leticia was in a dilemma. The divorce had been rough on her; her parents were religious and raised their three girls with strong Christian values. For the first thirteen years of Leticia's life, she thought her family life was good. The divorce was a surprise and resulted in her mother hating her dad and letting the girls know about it almost daily. Living with her mom resulted in less money in the household and more coping with her mom's extreme mood swings.

Dad married again a few years after the divorce. He and his wife had three more kids together. Leticia liked her stepmother but felt she was a little "too prissy" for her. She admitted that being at her dad and stepmom's home was a calmer environment, and she enjoyed her younger siblings. Leticia would have preferred to live with her dad and stepmom, but they lived further out in the country, and her mom lived in town. She loved her friends, and since she did not drive, she knew that staying with her mom gave her the opportunity to see her friends without depending on transportation.

Leticia had all the usual typical teen issues: dealing with puberty, peer groups, a boyfriend, classes, grades, appearance, and social media. At times, her mom would take her phone to punish her, and her dad would, consequently, be upset that he paid for her phone, and he thought his ex was overly punitive! Caught in the middle of two angry divorced parents, on top of the ups and downs of adolescence, and then living in two completely different types of families, with a blended family of two older teen girls and three half-siblings under the age of seven, was a lot of juggling for one teen. Life would have been much less complicated if she remained in her original family, but life constantly changes, and Leticia was coping with half-siblings, a stepmom, and two divorced parents whose anger toward each other always put her in the middle. She said that sleeping was a good way to avoid them and that cutting on herself relieved the pressure. Leticia was treated with antidepressants/anti-anxiety medicine and learned more coping strategies from

**our sessions together. Her parents were overwhelmed with the cutting but came to understand how their antagonistic behaviors toward each other were impacting her, along with adjusting to the divorce and stepfamily issues.**

You may be raising your teen as you are going through a divorce. The stress alone from the divorce can distract you from parenting your teen, as you are more stressed and having to attend to all the emotional and legal matters of divorce. Every member of your family will experience divorce differently. This is a situation when your cake can flip upside down.

**Divorce from your teen's perspective can be met with disgust, anger, and little sympathy, especially at first. Teens, especially younger ones, see life through a lens of black and white: "Why don't you guys go to counseling?", "Isn't marriage supposed to be forever?", or "Can't you two grow up and work it out?"**

**Or, they could shake their heads, clam up, and not say a thing. Teens are often so overwhelmed that they cannot influence the situation that they reluctantly resign themselves to the "oh, well, whatever" attitude. However, deep inside them, they are anxious and may put out a hyper-vigilant vibe, being extra tuned in to what is going on in the home: "Are Mom and Dad sleeping in different rooms?", "Is Mom crying? Are they fighting again?", "Is Dad going to be with us at Christmas?", or "Did I cause this because of my attitude?"**

These anxious thoughts may not be vocalized, especially since your teen may not be a frequent communicator with you. She can find lots of distractions: texting, social media, friends, and hanging out. She may not say much more to her friends than, "I think my parents are splitting up; it sucks." She may rationalize this when she gets the news that her parents are splitting: "Well, I'm not that surprised; plus, almost all my friends' parents are divorced."

You may find that your teen does not appear all that interested or emotional about your divorce; however, teens do need an outlet to talk about what is going on with them. Encouraging her to see a counselor or a caring adult she can trust can give her a safe emotional refuge to support her with what she is feeling and thinking. She could benefit from an objective adult to validate the adjustment process of divorce and to reassure her that her parents are still her parents during and after the split. Counselors can teach her to set boundaries, to discourage her parents from using her as a sounding board or pawn to use against each other.

> The wise parents will keep their kids out of the battles that can result from a bitter divorce. No matter how a parent feels about his or her spouse, it is important to remember that each parent is important to their teens. They share half of their DNA and want to love them both, without feeling guilty or disloyal.

You can communicate that the *behavior* your spouse may be engaged in (an affair, drinking, drugs, and violence) is the problem and that the parent is separate from the behavior. In other words, your teen should be encouraged to love and stay *safely* connected to her parents even when she does not approve of her parent's hurtful behavior(s). If the divorce has to do with the situation of growing apart and stagnation, it may be easier to be more positive about your ex: "Your dad is a great guy! I just somehow grew apart from him and can't seem to get back to where I need to be to stay in the marriage" or "Your mom is going through a lot and loves you very much; we both love you very much. Our divorce does not change our love for you or the fact that we are still your parents."

Many times, the impact of divorce that occurs when she is a teen can hit later in her adult life. As she has her own relationships, she can enter into them with the often-painful memories of knowing what breaking up can feel like. Consequently, she may have a more difficult time trusting the person whom she is with or that her relationship will last.

When your teen's world turns into an Upside-Down Cake, everything changes; the relationship with her parents, her physical home, surroundings, environment, family traditions, and often the way her parents behave. Sometimes, one parent (often the dad, as he tends to be the one that leaves home, whether he initiated the divorce or not) can be much less available. If there is an affair, for instance, and it is the dad who is involved, he may be so enthralled with seeing his girlfriend and, consequently, feel guilt and shame for what he is doing, that he may avoid his kids. Of course, this can be the same situation if the mom is involved in an affair. When feeling guilty and ashamed, people tend to avoid the people they are hurting. This, of course, is not always the case. In fact, there is never an *always the case* in divorce; each is unique while sharing the same stages of grief: denial, bargaining, depression, anger, and acceptance. Many parents are clear that staying involved and in contact with their kids is their priority during this challenging time.

This new situation can cause all kinds of emotional havoc. Using the example of the dad again (who lives away from the family home), he may want to take his kids for a traditional holiday to his parents' home. While the teen's mom is devastated, adjusting to the divorce, and feeling it is already too hard to cope, she is now faced with her ex wanting the kids for a holiday they all used to share. This leaves the teen in a position of adjusting to a holiday without one of her parents, where traditionally the family was always together. The teen can feel sorry or concerned about the parent left behind. When the cake is turned upside down, it leaves everyone hurting, adjusting, and having little emotional reserve to support anyone else. Some families may go on automatic pilot: "This is what we are going to do, so you need to deal with it," which results in stuffed feelings and resentment.

Teens now have to adjust to two separate homes. Many times, the parents will not live close to each other, a situation that causes its own adjustments for the teen. When visiting the other parent, your teen is now out of touch with her room, possessions, friends, and routines. Packing up to spend a weekend with Dad in a new town or state, with no friends and without her belongings can be challenging. She is at that stage of preferring to hang out with friends instead of her parents; therefore, it can put her in an aggravating bind.

While she does want to spend time with her parents, especially the one she doesn't see as much, it can be stressful and frustrating. Usually, she does not spend her weekends hanging out with her parents. Often, she lacks the courage to speak up: "Hey, Dad, I don't want to see you this weekend. I want to see my friends." Afraid of hurting her parent's feelings only compounds her suppressed feelings of wanting to do what she prefers to do, which is typically hanging out with her friends on the weekend.

> **Divorce is not only an emotional roller coaster ride, but it is also very inconvenient to kids. It can be a painful adjustment and a reminder that her family has changed because of how she feels around you. Many times, when visiting a parent, she can sense the sadness of that parent: "Mom seems so misplaced, and she looks so lonely in her new place" or "Without Mom around, Dad seems lost."**

When she is feeling sorry for one parent, she may then become upset with the other parent. Teens form all kinds of alliances and loyalties with their parents during this time. Teens seek balance and stability in their lives.

Feeling tossed around a bit, adjusting to the changes and all these new feelings can be too much. She has her own feelings about her parents' splitting up, and she can take on the feelings of her parents, whether it is anger toward one or sympathy for the other; her world as she knew it can just feel upside down and out of control.

## BE AWARE OF SIGNS THAT YOUR TEEN NEEDS EXTRA SUPPORT

Your teen may handle all this new stress by discovering the numbing effects of drug and alcohol use. This is unfortunate, but often typical, a collision between adolescence, divorce, and stress. Burying themselves in the world of drinking or drugs can provide immediate relief. And granted, there are plenty of situations where teens use drugs and alcohol when their home life is good, and there is no divorce. Parents cannot blame themselves for their teen's drug use during a divorce; however, it can be used as a way for your teen to not feel her feelings and to ignore the situation in order to cope. Teens may also cope by distancing, wanting to be away from home more, and seeking relief by being at a friend's house.

## WHAT YOU CAN DO

Getting professional help for the entire family is the best way to keep your Upside-Down Cake right side up. Counseling can be a support through all the grief and adjustment, giving each member of the family support during this often turbulent and painful time. There is life after divorce, but divorce is always hard on kids. If divorce is inevitable, then strive to do all you can to keep the situation focused on what is best for the kids.

Keeping your teens from the hostility or negative feelings you may have for your spouse is number one! Keeping in touch with your teens and not ignoring their need to be heard, loved, and the center of attention is crucial. The teen years are years of self-absorption and narcissism. The adolescent years are not supposed to be about the parents' personal lives.

The timing makes a difference. For example, if you are planning a divorce, and this is your teen's senior year in high school, consider postponing this until after he or she graduates. Surely, you can stay in your marriage for another year (of course, in instances of safety, this may not be possible). Focus on your teen's senior year so that this pivotal year is not impacted by the emotional attention a divorce takes on a family. Or wait until after December, to get through the holiday season as families are much more likely to be together and rely on traditions. Be conscious and aware that the timing of your split can be orchestrated. Of course, in your teen's world, there is never a good time to hear that his or her parents are splitting; it is always a painful adjustment. Time heals, and if handled sensitively with your kids' adjustment foremost in your mind, it can make a tough situation a bit easier on all.

Be extra sensitive when you do make those move-out changes. It is tough to watch the home being dismantled and losing the daily presence of a parent. Consider leaving your home intact at first. Do you really need to take the couch out of the main living room to furnish your new apartment? This leaves an empty space, which will remind your daughter of how much her life is changing when she walks in the room.

If an affair causes the divorce, do not introduce your teen to your new love. The last thing she wants is to adjust to you being giddy about a new person. She will not share the same delight as she watches everything familiar to her change. Better yet, give her a good year after the split before introducing her to a new romantic interest. She needs contact with just you, and she may not be pleased with your attention to a new person. Your teen can harbor deep resentment and feel betrayed. And she can feel even sorrier for the parent left behind who has no one. Help your kids adjust to your divorce slowly (at least a year or two) without introducing them to whom you are seeing. Giving them more time to adjust to the divorce will help them grow emotionally stronger. With more time to heal, they may take an interest in whom you are dating.

> If she is forced to meet your new friend and she knows that this person is the possible cause of the divorce, she may already have a negative attitude about that person. Do not add insult to injury by forcing her to meet this person and then, consequently, expecting her to be polite or even expecting her to enjoy them. Your excitement for your new love will not be met with her enthusiasm. Take these introductions very slowly; let time heal some wounds.

## THE GOOD NEWS

Your teen's world is flipped upside down because of the divorce; it is one of the most stressful situations a family can go through. However, life goes on, and most teens get through this very tough time and find their footing again. Be as sensitive and as available as you can for your teen. I know this may be asking a lot; navigating a divorce is a tremendous energy drain and a huge adjustment in your life. Adding extra counseling support can make this journey easier for all of you, it is indeed a situation in life where you all need additional support. Many adults had gone through a divorce as well when they were children or endured much more loss or grief throughout their lives over and above divorce. Never underestimate the resilience of humans to cope with loss, to grieve, to adjust, and to continue on. Teens I have worked with do best when at least one of their parents stays available to them, protects them from all the anger of divorce (often directed at the other parent), provides professional support, and, most of all, prioritizes their teen's needs before their own. This can be challenging, but crucial to your teen feeling secure, included and loved and not abandoned during this difficult adjustment. The Upside-Down Cake can be an unforeseen circumstance in one's life, but as with all unforeseen circumstances, this can be more successfully navigated with extra support, love, and open and honest communication.

# 15

# DOUBLE-LAYERED CAKE

## COPING WITH STEPFAMILIES

When your teen is coping with a Double-Layered Cake, it can double the stress from their family life. The first layer is the teen's parents. The second layer is when a parent is dating, or there are stepparents. Conflict and stress can double during these situations. It is only natural that, after a divorce, one or both parents will want to date again or eventually marry. There is nothing wrong with adults wanting to date and perhaps marry again. However, in the eyes of your teen, it is not so simple. But, if you keep in mind some basic practices and are aware of how your behaviors can impact your teen, things can go much better for your teen and you!

First off, the teen years are all about your teen, not you. Remember adolescence is a highly narcissistic and self-absorbed time of passage. Teens are focused on their bodies, self-image, appearance, their social lives, and are focused on being attracted to a possible girlfriend or boyfriend. The hormones are raging, and kids are sending out attraction signals all the time to one another. Your teen is typically interested in social activities, whether it is hanging out with friends, going to activities like sports, movies, or parties, using social media, or texting.

## HOW YOUR TEEN MAY BE FEELING

Your teen is focusing away from family and toward friends and independence. During adolescence, parents become more like shadow figures in their kids' lives; in the background, always lurking around, nagging them, and setting limits. Parents are busy with their own lives, which are often filled with work and responsibilities. Teens are not all that fascinated with your life, and, for the most part, they find your life rather tedious and boring. Friends offer them much more when it comes to fun, independence, and their deep need to socially belong.

> **When you are divorced and dating, your teen starts to pay more attention to whom you are dating. After all, you are getting all dressed up for your date. He observes you talking and texting with your love interest, and you seem "lame" in his eyes, laughing too much, talking flirtatiously, getting excited to go on a date. He finds this type of behavior quite annoying, and Heaven forbid, you are now affectionate with your new date. If you and your date are home and your son finds you cuddled up on the couch, it can make him uneasy: "Gross!" or "Why is Mom getting all dressed up, trying to look hot, and how can she stand that dude?"**

When parents date, teens are very observant of their parents' change in behavior. In addition, there is all the possible drama in the parent's life with a new relationship; the relationship can break up, and consequently, the parent is distraught. Or, perhaps, your teen started getting attached to this new person and then the relationship dissolved, upsetting your teen. In your teen's mind, dating is not normal for parents; dating is for teens and young adults.

If a new marriage is in the picture, he has to deal with a new authority figure around all the time. This can be a positive addition or a devastating addition that he has to cope with daily. On a more positive side, the new stepparent may be a much better mom or dad to him than his biological parent. He may begin to trust this person and enjoy having the attention he is getting from him or her. Or he may not like your new love in any way, shape or form. Being put in a daily situation with an adult he does not like, and whom you love, is very stressful for everyone. Sharing his home with someone he comes into contact with daily, eats dinner with, and hangs out with while watching TV is annoying. Also disturbing, is how his parent acts around this new love: "How can you possibly like this person? He acts like a total moron," or "She is so annoying!"

Sometimes, your teen can see right through your new love better than you can. Love and attraction can influence someone's judgment. Your teen may have been right all along about the character of the person you brought into his life. He suppresses his feelings, wondering how you can be so blind and, at the same time, is protective of you: "Why do you let him treat you like that? Weren't we better off when you were single without this guy hanging around all the time?"

## AND, THOSE STEPKIDS

No matter when you add the extra layer to your family's cake, it doubles the number of people (authority figures) your teen has to deal with. And if the teen has stepparents on both sides of the family, it is even more challenging. To complicate matters even more, stepparents can bring in children of their own, blending both families. He may never be all that thrilled about the new siblings in his life: "No I do not think little Justin is cute; he is annoying!"

If the new siblings are also teens, this can be a setup for a more serious situation. At this age, hormones run strong, and with a mix of unrelated teens in the home, an attraction or crush can form, resulting in stepsiblings going too far and becoming sexually involved. A sixteen-year-old girl having access to a seventeen-year-old boy who is not blood-related can create a situation right under the roof that parents can miss or be in denial about. Extra supervision is needed, which can be challenging when parents work and teens are left alone.

**Teens do not like friends imposed on or picked out for them; imagine having to be related to or live with stepsiblings daily?**

Some families pull this off beautifully, creating blended families who are loving, protective, fair, safe, supportive, and for the most part, everyone thrives in the new family. However, for many more, the stepparent may not like your kids (and vice versa) or may have more objectivity when raising the stepchildren and subjectivity when raising his or her own. Also, the newly added teens may bring in problematic new behaviors, attitudes, drugs, or alcohol that your teen had not previously been exposed to. This creates conflict between the parent and his or her new love as well each parents' style of parenting. The parents can disagree when raising their kids and, consequently, feel they have to choose between their new partner and their kids.

## SOME STRESS SIGNALS YOUR TEEN MAY GIVE YOU

Teens are focused on their own lives when growing up and not on dealing with new parents that come into their lives. These changes in their adolescent years can be overwhelming. Feeling overwhelmed as a teen often presents as: withdrawing, being angry, having a bad attitude, avoiding parents, making rude comments, using passive-aggressive behaviors, being depressed, and using substances.

It is a good idea to have your teen see a counselor during his teen years, especially when he is adjusting to major changes in the family system. He could use the support of a safe and objective professional who can hear him out, validate how he feels and thinks about the situation, and give him tools and suggestions for coping with his new family. The counselor can also help the parents become more aware of the impact of new and blended families on their child and help the family navigate the situation much more effectively and harmoniously.

## WHAT YOU CAN DO TO HELP

Teens usually prefer and are quite satisfied with, the first layer on the cake. Adding an extra layer means much more cake than they ever wanted to eat. Seek the help of a professional, read articles and books on step parenting, and provide an environment where your teen is the focus of these years instead of your new marriage. Often, the reason most second marriages fail is the struggles and adjustments when dealing with step-parenting and the stressors that go with all of this adjusting.

> **Seek support to ease the transition and adjustment. Stay focused as well as you can on your teen and his life, being sure that your child can truthfully communicate with you. Have him be honest with how he feels about your new partner without getting defensive, angry, or minimizing his true feelings or defending your new love.**

Often in time, teens come around to attach to their new parent. Keep in mind that your feelings toward your new love are nowhere near your teen's feelings. Time can help or aggravate your new relationship. Either way, this is a challenging situation, especially for teens. Let him set his own pace for accepting his new family members.

## THE GOOD NEWS

If you are sensitive and measured about the impact of dating or a new marriage during your teen's adolescence, you will be far more successful than if you do things too soon and pressure your child to accept the situation when your teen is not ready. My best advice after a divorce is to wait a good year before introducing anyone you may be dating to your kids. Save your dating life for when your kids are with the other parent. After the second year, and if you are now serious about whom you are dating, introduce your person to your kids, outside of your home, perhaps at lunch or dinner. Keep it relaxed, not pushy, and save any display of affection for another time. Your kids will not find your date as impressive as you do.

After the first meeting, genuinely listen to your kids' feedback. Don't argue or try to change their minds. Let them know that you understand that they may not want anything to do with your new love, but that you have found someone important to you, and that you hope they will keep an open mind (and, of course, you are also juggling your new love's feelings about your kids).

Take things slowly. Eventually, during that second year, invite your date into your home for dinner, but do not rush a sleep over. You having someone other than their parent sleeping with you is not a thought your kids want to entertain. Save it for at least a year after your kids get to know your new love. By pacing your kids for a good two years after a divorce, and gradually letting them get used to your new partner, you set yourself and your new love up for success.

Many teens begin to trust and enjoy a new adult parent figure in their lives. Some may enjoy them much more than their own parent, especially if their parent has had major problems or has abandoned them after the divorce. Learning to trust other adults can be a very positive experience for your teen. Just be sure your teen knows *you* are in charge of them, *not* your new love. They know that you are their parent and will respect your authority long before someone else's, so it is up to you to do the heavy lifting (and this is something you should clue your new person into, also).

Many successful families have not only blended but are grateful for their new larger and extended family. Blended families are more common these days, and teens are aware that parents can divorce and remarry. I have seen blended families create love and acceptance, and consequently, blended families who have not blended at all, causing stress for everyone. If you remember that there was an original family, (which are your kids, you and your ex) long before the second family (or third, or fourth...), and you respect your teen's need to belong to this original family over and above belonging to the stepfamily, things will go so much smoother. So many times, teens are blended into a new family, and their original family is rarely acknowledged which can diminish the importance and value that this original family once served. While you will want your children to treat your new love with respect, your kids were there first, before your new person. Your teen wants you to remember that and to be on their team and advocate, love, and take the best care of them over and above anyone else in your life. If you do that, you have a much better chance of successfully fitting together all of the pieces in your new life.

# 16

## CUPCAKES

### PREGNANCY

I met my new client, Carly, at the end of her ninth-grade year. She seemed to have a good life at home with her mom and stepdad. Her dad lived nearby and was involved in her life, so she felt close to both of them. Carly's mom wanted her to come to counseling because her grades were dropping, and her mom felt Carly was spending too much time with her boyfriend. Mom thought that her daughter might need someone to talk to who could help her make better choices.

In our second session, Carly told me she was very much in love with her eighth-grade boyfriend and that they had, in fact, had sex. I asked her about birth control, and she said they were not using any. I, of course, advised her that this was a considerable risk, and since her mom was supportive and open, she should talk to her about getting on birth control. We also discussed all of the consequences of what pregnancy could mean to her life and her boyfriend at such a young age. Carly was 15 and her boyfriend 14, much too young to deal with a pregnancy.

In our third session, Carly announced that she was pregnant. I was taken aback, even though, of course, I knew this was a very real outcome of unprotected sex. She had told her mom, and they had scheduled an obstetrics appointment. Carly was determined to keep and raise the baby, and mom was supportive and on board to help. By the time Carly was four months pregnant, she had dropped out of high school and quit all of her sports teams. She had been an athlete and loved soccer, volleyball, and softball. She lived at home and did online schooling. A few girlfriends would text her and visit, but her social life grew more and more isolated. Much to her boyfriend's credit, he stuck by her side, though he could not provide any financial support due to his age and his parents' lack of resources. Carly ended her counseling as it was getting more difficult to get to our appointments. To this day, I do not know how she is doing as a young mother. She was fortunate to have loving support from home, though her baby tremendously impacted her parents' lifestyle as well.

Your teen daughter may find herself in a situation where she is now a mother in the family and baking her own little Cupcake. At first, you may be completely in denial that this could be happening to you. There was no plan to bake Cupcakes! How could this possibly have happened? When you discover that your teen is pregnant, it is a big deal! Depending on her age, it is a complicated situation, especially if she is under sixteen. Your child, now pregnant, being so young and dependent, can seriously and negatively impact her and the child's future. If your teen is over sixteen, it is obviously still a big deal, especially since you almost had her raised; but now a Cupcake comes along, threatening all of your plans for your daughter. If you are the parents of the son who helped make the Cupcake, you, too, will be overwhelmed, shocked, and worried about your son's future. Of course, this becomes a family crisis, one that is often taken care of very privately at first. This is not something that you, a soon-to-be grandparent, shares on social media. You may hide the pregnancy from your spouse, realizing how upset he or she will be when he or she finds out. In our culture, there is little benefit when your teen adds a Cupcake to the family.

> **Three choices immediately present themselves; the only three options that a teen pregnancy automatically generates: abortion, adoption, or raising the child.**

All of these choices come with their own pain, consequences, and plan of action. Often, parents jump first to terminating the pregnancy. Even parents who are against pro-choice ideals and are adamantly against abortion may find themselves advocating strongly for the termination option. Realizing how young their teen is, how this will complicate and possibly ruin her future, and, at the very least, how this will make life more difficult for all involved, can result in desperation to fix the situation. And if the family does not like the father, there is even more reason to lean toward termination.

If you are the parent of the baby's dad, you might advocate for abortion as the best option. This pregnancy may result with consequences of your son having minimal contact with his child (as well as his extended family) and his being more of an outsider than actively involved in raising his child. There are also the financial costs for support and medical bills he will have to pay throughout his teen and adult years.

**There is enough blame to go around from each parent:**

- "How could he do this to my daughter?"
- "Why did she let herself get pregnant and trap our son?"
- "Why wasn't she on birth control?"
- "Why didn't he use protection?"
- "I trusted my daughter to stay a virgin. He must have pressured her."
- "I knew I shouldn't have let you two spend so much time together!"
- "What will people think?"
- "Oh my gosh, your grandmother is going to have a heart attack over this, she will never understand!"
- "And me, what about me? I am certainly too young to be a grandparent! I am not changing my life to raise your child!"
- "This is ruining your future!"
- "What were you thinking?"

Hence, terminating the pregnancy often becomes the primary choice.

"Let's take care of this now, before you are too far along. And, then, young lady, you are staying away from this boy!"

Or, if abortion is not an option, there is adoption. This option will not hide the pregnancy. Your daughter and the father will go through the entire nine months, and everyone will know. Your daughter can risk harassment, teasing, doors closing (difficult to play sports at nine-months pregnant), public ridicule, and loss of friends. As her parent, you risk embarrassment, silently bearing this burden, and feeling quite alone. Parents are anxious and afraid of what their daughter may be facing every day as she goes to school, perhaps the only pregnant student at the school. Your son, especially depending on the relationship: one-night stand, casual relationship, or his girlfriend, is given a bad time with his peers, embarrassed (especially if this was a random sexual encounter), and stressed on top of everything else at school.

You see your daughter's body change and are concerned for her health, especially if there are any complications. She gains weight, is more emotional, has mood swings, and is outcast from her regular social group. There are always those friends who stick by her, but usual shopping trips to the mall have a new meaning. When your daughter can only shop in maternity and her size four friends are hitting the current fashion stores, socializing can become awkward. Your daughter may be left out of many normal activities; certainly, sports is one that will go. Hanging out at parties around drinking and other assortments of drugs won't feel right. Even driving around in cars or sitting in movie theaters can become too uncomfortable.

And, then, there is the attachment to her baby, which is natural during pregnancy. Your daughter sees her body changing, begins to feel the baby move and sees her baby on the ultrasound. You also are a witness to these developments and realize that this is your grandchild, a new member of your family. As you grow attached, you have daydreams of having this baby around combined with your fears of what this child will mean to your daughter's life and yours, if you do decide to keep this baby. This is a very emotionally stressful and painful time for all.

> Most likely, if you are choosing adoption, you both will be actively involved with an organization that helps with the details—the legal end, the search for the right adoptive parents, and other details needed to complete the adoption.

You, your daughter, and the dad's side of the family may all be interviewing the potential parents. All of this is bittersweet, but all agree that this is the best choice for the teens and the baby; finding stable, financially secure parents who are ready to raise a child and give their child the best life possible. You know that this frees your teen to go back to her previous life and hit the resume button.

However, there can be some painful surprises along the way. Perhaps, the parents of the teen dad want to raise the baby and do not want this adoption. This may be another source of pain to the girl's parents, to know the boy's parents could raise the baby. Especially if the girl's parents do not like his family and worry about how the baby will be raised. And if they do like his family, it can hit too close to home. To know your daughter's baby is in the same community, where you will run into the family who is raising her child, can be too much. It may be far easier emotionally to choose the parents outside of both families, have the baby live elsewhere, and if it is an open adoption, get periodic progress reports or visit the child every once in a while.

Either way, watching your daughter hand her Cupcake over after nine months to the new parents is emotionally painful, an ambivalent situation, but knowing that this chapter is over and that the baby is in great hands is a huge relief. Leaving the hospital for home without the Cupcake that you and your family spent so many months caring for during pregnancy is a mix of grief, relief, and second-guessing your choice. And if you are the parents of the son, you can feel the same way, that this untimely pregnancy was a painful emotional journey. Even though choosing that this was the right thing to do for all, to carry this baby to full term but then give the baby to loving adoptive parents still hurts. Throughout the life of this child, both parents and grandparents will at times think, "He may be eighteen now and graduating from high school, and what if he finds us? What will we tell him?"

However, for now, it is time to get back to the teen years—on to less serious matters. And it is time to be sure your daughter or son is well-covered for birth control.

And then there is that third choice: raising the Cupcake, choosing to go the marathon, the pregnancy, the permanent interruption of a normal teen life. Also, depending on how young your child is (parent at thirteen, a parent at sixteen, etc.), you are in for a long haul. As the parents of the daughter, you will most likely bear most of the responsibility for the dependent care of both.

As the parents of the son, you will bear financial responsibility and may want access to your grandchild. The teens being too young to marry, there are legal issues such as medical bills, child support, and a parenting plan to work out with the mother's family.

Your teen will most likely get on public assistance to help out with medical bills, food stamps, WIC (Women of Infants and Children) diapers and formula, and day-care expenses. If you do not want to go that route, you, as a parent, will be providing most or all of these needed items and planning where the baby will fit in at home while navigating your daughter's continued schooling. Your daughter may stay home to raise her child because she is unable to afford daycare. Your daughter may miss out on typical school activities, such as attending dances, homecoming, prom, sports events, assemblies, and other teen activities to care for her baby. School can be put off or changed to an online school or alternative school.

As your grandchild grows, your home becomes lively with this Cupcake around; it is back to baby-proofing, car seats, sleepless nights, food thrown off the high chair, and so on. And you will do your fair share of childcare, supporting your daughter to get back to some form of a typical teen social life. You will painfully watch as your daughter becomes more socially isolated—getting fewer texts asking her to go out or spend the night with friends. Not too many teens want a car seat with them and a baby to put up with on an outing. A one-year-old at a movie is not exactly an enjoyable experience that allows you to be absorbed in the film.

If you are the parents of the son, you may now have a baby in your home every other weekend. While your son may be enthralled and loving toward his little Cupcake, he may not have the best parenting skills. Consequently, you may find yourselves watching your grandchild on his weekend. Your son has sports games to attend, girls to date, and boys to hang with. It is not likely that the teen parents' relationship will continue due to stress, pressure, conflict, and just being too young. Your son may be paying child support, which means that if he works, his wages can be garnished by the State, especially if the mother is getting welfare. Child support is a costly continuing obligation until the child is eighteen. That is a lot to ask of an often minimum-wage employee.

> **There is life after these three choices: adoption, abortion, or raising the baby, and there have been many successful, positive outcomes with all of these difficult choices.**

Is it all that surprising that you find a Cupcake in your life? We are biologically driven to reproduce. Centuries ago, we did not live very long, maybe thirty years, if one was lucky. Sex and pregnancy were normal in the adolescent years. Menstruation begins in the teen years or younger, and menstruation prepares the body for reproduction. Testosterone levels are high. It is normal and natural to have a strong sexual drive in the teen years when bodies are young, strong, healthy, and ready to produce offspring. We are all here from our ancestors' teen pregnancies. It was the norm, natural and accepted.

As our society grew more agricultural and industrial, we lived longer lives and had more time to reproduce and raise children. Adolescent sexual urges were suppressed and forbidden, whether through religious beliefs or family morals. Birth control was not available for teens for the most part. With the more mainstream emergence of Planned Parenthood in the 1960s, teens could, at least, without parent permission, obtain birth control and treatment for sexually transmitted diseases. However, regardless that there is more availability of birth control, sexually active teens often use nothing at all.

Teens can be in denial that sex leads to pregnancy. This is a conversation I had with one sixteen-year-old client:

"You are telling me that you and your boyfriend are having unprotected sex, and you have been for the last seven months?" I asked.

"Yep," the teen replied.

"Don't you think that it is only a matter of time before you get pregnant? I mean, it is a miracle you haven't gotten pregnant up to this point," I said.

"I know! We are pretty sure that I can't get pregnant, so we aren't worried," the teen replied.

"Really how is that?" I asked.

"Well, because we have been having sex for over seven months, and I have not gotten pregnant yet, so we are pretty sure it won't happen. Obviously, something about our bodies keeps me from getting pregnant," the teen replied.

"Hmm, may not be true. I think what is most likely true is you two have been extremely lucky! I highly suggest you both do the responsible thing, and you get on the pill, and he uses condoms."

She did not buy into this suggestion. She delivered her little girl Cupcake in May of her senior year. She lives with her single mom. The father stayed until after their daughter was born. He is now living a life without either of them. This is often the sad outcome of adolescent pregnancies and parenthood.

Another young woman I had worked with since she was a teen, but was now a freshman in college had become sexually active with her twenty-three-year-old boyfriend. She was also not using birth control. When I questioned her about birth control, she said, "No we haven't been using any."

"OK, you are smart enough to know that sex leads to pregnancy! You are a freshman in college. Do you want a baby right now in your life?" I asked.

"Heaven's no!" she said. "Please stop saying this you are freaking me out!"

As if me bringing up the thought that pregnancy can result from sex was so off her radar that the idea of it terrified her. She never used birth control. She delivered her first-born little girl Cupcake in her sophomore year of college.

It is interesting that with all of the resources available for birth control, many teens do not use them or accept responsibility for the consequences of being sexually active.

I have worked with one teen who refreshingly said, "I have been with my boyfriend for a year. We both agreed that sex is too risky. We do not want to be teen parents, so we abstain." When these teens were together for their second year, she knew they were headed for a sexual relationship. She went to her doctor and got on the pill. He used condoms. They were mature and responsible especially when they both were just seventeen. Of course, this is the best precaution (outside of abstinence) to prevent teen pregnancy. Also, with the low dose of birth control these days and the possibility of a pin-size hole in a condom, pregnancy can still occur. However, those precautions are available and always the best choice if the choice is to be sexually active.

> Parents, a word of caution here: no matter what your choice is with your pregnant daughter, it is your teen who has the final say. This can leave you frustrated, angry, anxious and feeling powerless.

If your teen refuses an abortion, you cannot make her have one. Even if she is legally your responsibility, you can end up in a tense power struggle trying to get her into the doctor and force an abortion. Teens who have had their parents pressure them to have an abortion often suffer emotionally. I have worked with young teens who resent their parents and grieve for the baby they did not choose to abort. If your daughter wants to give her baby up for adoption or keep her baby, (in many states parents have total or some authority over this) forcing her to make this tough decision may result in many painful arguments, tears, pleading, and so on when dealing with your daughter's decision to cope with her pregnancy.

Ultimately, your teen will make the decision. And if she reluctantly complies with your wishes, she can suppress deep anger and grief, since it was not her choice. It is a good idea to have your teen get professional support, someone who is more objective and not emotionally tied to the outcome. Moreover, I would suggest the same for you. Having someone to sort through all of your mixed emotions and fears can provide the extra support needed in this time of crisis.

## YOU ARE NOT ALONE

If you are faced with your teen's pregnancy, realize that there are a lot of sexually active teens in middle and high school. Your teen was not the only teen engaging in this activity; she was unfortunately, the one who ended up making a Cupcake.

While pregnancy is stressful and a significant disruption to the teen years, life goes on. Neither of the three choices are easy to deal with, and all will emotionally impact your family's life. Abstinence is always the smartest choice; abstinence keeps everyone from dealing with these three painful choices: abortion, adoption, or raising the baby. Many teens have their first sexual experience without birth control, and many end up pregnant the first time. There is no evidence that putting your teen on birth control implies that he or she has permission to have sex. Teens do not actively seek sex just because they get on the pill. However, if you support her in getting birth control before she becomes sexually active, then pregnancy prevention is in place.

## YOUR SON IS AT RISK

For boys, until there is male birth control, carrying and using condoms is all they have to at least help prevent unwanted pregnancy and sexually transmitted diseases (STDs) when abstinence is not the choice of the moment.

There is also date rape. Sadly, this is an under-reported trauma many young girls suffer through alone. Girls risk gossip and group pressure if they disclose who raped them. When teens gather, often without adults on site, and then isolate, and add alcohol or substance use, then the risk for girls for unwanted sex increases. Date rape is a secret many teens keep to themselves with a serious emotional price. And if a pregnancy results from rape, this drastically complicates a teen's life.

> **Talk to your son about consent. It is the responsibility of boys to get consent before having sex (without pressuring, coercing, or threatening). Talk with them about all of the consequences of having sex and the emotional impact on both your son and the girl. If there is alcohol involved, this increases the risk that your son did not get consent for sex from an intoxicated girl. Was she able to make a clear choice regarding having sex with him?**

Males are at risk for a rape charge, especially if there is alcohol involved. In many of today's courts, if two teens are drinking and end up having sex, and then later the girl realizes that she should not have been in that situation, that the alcohol clouded her judgment, and she feels she did not consent with a clear head, she can make a case for rape. Previously, the courts would often turn their back on rape allegations when two teens were drinking with a "well, serves you right, you two shouldn't have been drinking" attitude. Often, it is her word against his word. These days the pendulum has swung the other way: if both teens had been drinking, the courts may assume that the girl could not have consented as she was not in her "right mind" and that the boy took advantage of her. If this girl decides she made a bad choice or the alcohol clouded her judgment and her parents back her, your son can, in fact, be charged with rape. Talk to your sons, let them know the risks, and encourage them to be smart when it comes to having sex. Coach them to be sure the girl is someone they know well, that the relationship is, in fact, a consenting relationship, and that no always means no.

## THE GOOD NEWS

It is a fact of life that teens will be interested in sex, and no matter what you tell them or how much you keep an eye on them, there is always the possibility your teen will engage in sexual activity. If you are aware of this, you can educate your teen, whether son or daughter, on using birth control methods and avoiding risky sexual experiences. Educate your teen about various birth control options; your doctor or Planned Parenthood will be happy to help with this. Talk to your sons about the risk to them if there is any sign of non-consensual sex and the risks of alcohol or drug use and sex. It is not too early to begin these conversations.

With prevention, you will stand a much greater chance of preventing an unwanted pregnancy and having to deal with all of the tough choices a teen pregnancy brings forth. Abstinence is the only guaranteed way to avoid pregnancy, and sharing that message with your teen is always a good reminder. But also, being realistic about the possibility that your child will choose to have sex during the teen years will hopefully motivate you to have open and honest discussions with your teen. Teen pregnancy is preventable, and, fortunately, we have so many birth control options available today.

And, when raising teens, there is always the possibility that you may be surprised to find a Cupcake in your life. Get professional help and support if you are facing this situation. You will need it, and it can make the journey a bit less overwhelming.

# LIGHTER INGREDIENTS

# 17

## ANGEL FOOD

### SHINING STAR

Tiana came to counseling due to her relationship ending after two years. She was in the middle of her senior year, and she wanted to have the freedom to pursue a college life without being tied to her high school boyfriend. Her boyfriend was a year younger, and she felt they were fighting more, and it was time to end the relationship. She seemed to be as respectful as she could toward him, but she still wanted some support to be sure she was doing the right thing. Tiana's parents were lucky to have such a thoughtful and emotionally intelligent girl. She was their first-born, class president, popular, friendly, and a 4.0 student. She had aspirations of either being a pediatrician or an obstetrician. She had a great sense of humor, and she fit well into any social group at school. She was kind and often her teachers' favorite. Tiana earned money to help buy her car, took great care of it, and had worked at a local business since she was a sophomore. Her dad was a doctor, and her mom stayed home and raised their three children. Her parents were

**humble and grateful for their eldest daughter. They took no credit for how exceptional she was when it came to making good choices and excelling at school. They were thrilled that they got so lucky—proud parents of an easy-to-raise daughter. They were the lucky ones who managed to raise a daughter from birth to high school graduation without a bump in the road!**

Ah, an Angel Food Cake—soft, fluffy, and sweet. If you are the lucky parents who are baking an Angel Food Cake, you will have minimal, if any, trouble! Some families are fortunate enough to get one Angel Food Cake per family; some families only bake Angel Food Cakes, though most do not get through the teen years without tasting the other specialty cakes. If you are one of the lucky ones who baked an Angel Food Cake, you should be jumping for joy!

**These Angels are a breeze to raise. As teens they are intrinsically motivated by their own will and choices, having very little to do with what their parents extrinsically do to motivate them.**

For example, this teen will manage her schoolwork, meet deadlines, and work for straight As. Her parents do not need to ask her about homework or monitor her grades; their daughter provides all the motivation to do her best in school. This Angel Food Cake can also juggle many balls: participate in many sports, clubs, activities, have an active social life, and even have a relationship, while successfully managing it all. While occasionally you see a frustrated attitude or irritability, for the most part, she is easy to live with, amicable, and she manages her middle and high school years with ease and accomplishment. She has an internal moral compass that motivates her to make good choices.

Self-motivated teens are usually clear that they do not want to drink or use drugs. Also, even if they do try drinking or drugs, they typically do not continue, often ending up being the designated driver for their friends or avoiding all social situations where people are "partying." These Angel Cakes need minimal discipline and respond to family norms and expectations as if all of these teen years are a piece of cake.

If you have an Angel Cake, who does need a bit of parental, extrinsic motivation, for example, you occasionally have to remind her about homework, have high expectations, and will give consequences for out-of-line behaviors; you still find your teen will comply as she respects you and your rules. She knows what your expectations are and follows them. There may be a part of her that wants to rebel, however, she has a healthy respect for you and wants to avoid negative consequences and prefers to stay on a good path.

At times the influence of religion can motivate a teen to stay on the Angel side of cake. Being a part of a church and related activities can provide a spiritual code, which keeps teens on the path of making good choices. However, this is not one of those ingredients added to the cake mix that guarantees an Angel Cake. Teens often question the religion they are raised in during adolescence, challenging it or rejecting it. And even those teens who are involved in their church community can end up being tempted to hang out with the Rum Cakes, Brownies, or Devil Food Cakes; they may Have Their Cake and Not Eat It Too, deal with an Upside-Down Cake, and so on. Adolescence is a time of risk-taking, providing more freedom and the desire to be away from the parents' radar. Many times, teens raised within a religious family will re-choose their family's religion later in life if they do reject or balk at it in the teen years. However, religion can influence a teen's moral compass and provide opportunities for a teen to participate in healthy activities within their church or organization.

Raising an Angel Food Cake is a beautiful experience for parents! To enjoy your child through these often-turbulent years while your friends are pulling out their hair is a gift. Most parents who are raising such teens often say that they have no idea what they have done to have such a great kid! They admit that their teen has always been a joy to raise. These parents get many rewarding experiences from their teens: watching them excel in sports, perhaps being voted as class president, becoming valedictorian or student of the month for academic achievement and good citizenship and so on, and their high GPA means they can apply to a variety of colleges they would like to attend. You may hear great feedback from teachers and coaches on what a pleasure it is to have your teen in their classes and on their teams. Your daughter may even juggle a job during high school where her employer thinks the world of her. She manages to save money for college or a car and helps contribute to the expenses of her teen years.

Just like parents who raise the other varieties of Cakes, the parents who raise Angel Food Cakes are not always sure just what ingredients they added to get the cake to bake so perfectly. You can put in all the right ingredients to create a successful teen, and still, the outcome is not 100 percent predictable.

> **Consequently, while the parents who struggle with difficult teen situations should not blame themselves, the parent who did not struggle at all should be careful not to take all the credit. Teens will turn out to be who they are and make their own choices, regardless of your recipe, your ingredients, and your wishes.**

Yes, you can have a positive or negative impact on her home environment. Yes, you can do mostly all the right things, mostly all the wrong things, or somewhere in between. However, teens in some of the worst circumstances (often ending up in foster care due to parental abuse or neglect) or teens in the best situations (stable, loving, and safe upbringing) can end up being a desirable Angel Food Cake. You really can never predict how great your Cake is going to turn out. So, put a smile on your face and breathe a sigh of relief and relax, as you got lucky and baked an Angel!

## THE GOOD NEWS

It's all good news!

# 18

## CARROT CAKE

### THE SMALL STUFF

Hailey came to counseling as an eighth grader, holding a stuffed purple dinosaur. She also wore slippers and an Avengers t-shirt. Hailey's mom felt she was isolating too much, refusing to go to school and was worried about where her daughter's school anxiety was coming from. Hailey was shy at first but warmed up to me as we got to know each other. Hailey was creative, loved to draw, and often came dressed in different clothing styles as well as hairstyles. Her outfits were often mismatched and carefree. She considered herself a combination of "punk and Goth." She had a small clique of friends, and she described them as the "outsiders." They claimed that they accepted everyone, but that very few accepted them.

During Hailey's high-school years, she would see me a few times each year to touch base about some issues, usually involving her friends, boyfriend, or parents. Her style changed throughout the years; sometimes she looked like a Catholic school girl dressed in plaid skirts, white shirts, and braids; other times sporty with a baseball hat, cropped pants, and t-shirts. She had been a vegetarian but then changed to a diet of chicken nuggets and pepperoni pizza. Being an analytical thinker, she liked to talk about metaphysical topics as well as social issues, gender issues, racism and was a huge animal rights advocate (much to the dismay of her parents, as she often brought home stray pets).

She had several changes of taste in music over the years: punk, metal, country, techno, and classical. What was consistent was that Hailey was a creative person and loved trying on many different identities and expressing her many selves. As an only child, her parents indulged her and did not push back with restrictions. She maintained an average GPA, tried pot and drinking, but was not all that interested. She preferred drawing, hanging with her boyfriend, and spending a lot of time alone. Her parents were proud of her, but at times were exhausted from coping with many of her ongoing changes. Hailey was consistently inconsistent, and since she stayed away from the harmful risky teen behaviors, her parents were willing to settle for constantly adjusting to all her changes.

One thing for sure about the teen years is that they are rarely dull or predictable. You raise your child in the same way you always have, and the next thing you know you have a teen sitting at the dinner table saying, "Oh, by the way, I'm a vegetarian now, and so I am not eating meat." She can announce this with quite a lot of conviction and pride. After you have put a lovely dinner on the table, your teen now decides to take a spoonful of potatoes and turns her nose up at the mere sight of the beef.

Of course, there are the typical family member reactions:

Dad: "Oh, for heaven's sake, I have been eating meat for dinner every day of my life, and you say there's something wrong with that?"

Mom "If God didn't want us to eat meat, he wouldn't have created cows and chickens."

Mom: "You need meat so you get enough protein and iron, especially during puberty. You could get anemic and sick. This is not a good idea."

Siblings: "Ha-ha, a vegetarian, you are so dumb; always some weirdo thing with you."

And, still, your teen can be quite opinionated and determined: "That's fine; you guys can say all you want. However, I do not believe in killing animals. Do you even know how they torture that cow that you are all putting in your mouths? It's horrible, and I, for one, am not going to take part in such cruelty." Or, some teens when asked why they have suddenly decided to become vegetarians will not have a clue; it just seems like a good idea to them, and they stick to it. Perhaps, they even become a vegan (no animal products at all, eggs, milk, butter, leather clothing, etc.). Some can share facts about why they have made this choice. Some do not have a lot of reasons other than it is just fun to proclaim it; it inconveniences the family norm, and it raises eyebrows, which can be satisfying by itself for a teen.

When your teen is trying on all kinds of new identities from vegetarian, vegan, prep, hipster, Goth, gamer, stoner, whatever the latest identity is, you may find yourself anywhere from annoyed to infuriated. Teens are notorious for exploring new identities, from clothing styles, hairstyles, piercings, tattoos, and hanging out with different peer groups, to having rebellious attitudes and opinions.

This period of life is one of finding her way, developing an identity that is against the status quo, and it can create shockwaves in her family when she is trying to find a peer group. Most of these identities will be a thing of your daughter's past as she grows older. Some of her experimentation can be more permanent, such as tattoos and piercings; some are temporary such as hair and clothing. As a parent, keeping up with these changes can be challenging; disapproving of the changes can be normal, after all, this is not how you raised her (which is often her point as she moves to more personal autonomy and independence from her family).

This is a time in your parenting life to remember that this, too, shall pass and not to sweat the small stuff.

Some styles your daughter adopts could be more disconcerting. Some of the Goth, emo, or gang identities can indicate some depression and anger expressed with darker clothing or a more anti-establishment attitude and can suggest violent thoughts or behaviors. This is certainly not always the case, but it is worth paying attention to and not ignoring. The same would be with a hippie or stoner image affiliated with possible drug use. Once again, you cannot always judge a book by its cover. Athletes can use as much or more alcohol and drugs than non-athletes, even though there is a misconception that if you keep your kids in sports, they won't turn to drugs.

## GOOD NEWS

Teens are immersed in the years of searching for an identity. Your daughter will try on a variety of new images, identities, and new ways of behaving. As the parent of a Carrot Cake, go along with as many of her new identities as you can tolerate. Most of these changes do not last all that long, though some may stick, so you get to choose your battles. With other things to be concerned about: drugs, drinking, sex, driving, and school achievement, when stages like this come along, remember that you are dealing with Carrot Cake; delicious and, for the most part, harmless compared to the many other Cakes discussed in this book.

# FROSTING
# YOUR CAKE

# 19

## KEEP YOUR CAKE
## FROM FALLING

### Be Smarter than the Situation

You have now tasted the many Cake varieties you may find yourself baking as a parent of a teen. You realize that the innocence of your child's grade school years is long gone. And if you are raising more than one child, you may have baked several of these different Cakes at one time or another or even combined a few of them. Each teen is unique. All teens have their unique DNA, family, and social and environmental influences.

> There is no predicting, no matter how you raise your teens, how they are going to cope with their adolescent years and then transition to their adult life. However, you do have 100 percent control over how you choose to parent and raise your teen; this is your circle of influence.

Parent the best that you know how, learn what you can, listen to your gut, heart, and mind, and get support when you start to feel like you forgot how to parent. It takes a lot of personal strength to parent through the teen years. It is not easy in most cases. Parents can suffer from a mild form of PTSD (posttraumatic stress disorder), in some cases for years, after their child's adolescence ends. They still shudder when they think of what those years were like and how grateful they are now that those years are behind them.

Since you emotionally operate from the two primary positions of love and fear, at times, you might feel you have lost your rational mind. Occasionally, you may spew out words to your teen that you thought you would never hear yourself say, often repeating words that your parents said to you and that you vowed you would never say to your kids. The stakes are high for your own emotions and sanity when you love your child so much and are afraid of all those things that can hurt him or her during the risk-taking adolescent years.

Consequently, parenting your teen can be very frustrating, especially when you are trying to get your teen to change a behavior, whether that is to be successful at school, to stop using alcohol and drugs, to stop seeing that boy/girl you do not like, to change his or her attitude or style of clothing, or whatever else you are concerned about.

My work with teens has taught me that they tend to change their behavior more for a reward than for punishment. I have worked with many parents who have grounded their teens for life or taken away their phones, computers, cars, video games, and any other item meaningful to them. Moreover, in return, they often get a teen who could care less about caring: "it doesn't seem like anything we try changes anything, like our teen, is in a *whatever, who cares?* state of apathy." Parents give up, not knowing what else they are supposed to do to get their teen back on the right path.

A more punitive consequence may only result in a deeper power struggle. Your teen will make it a game of willpower; who will hold out the longest without breaking? I have known teens who isolate themselves in their rooms for hours: no phone, no television, no computer, nothing, and they will communicate the unspoken message: *Do whatever you want; I am not going to cooperate.*

There are logical consequences, which should be used when possible, but not when you and your teen are in a heated argument. For instance, if you have an expectation of when your teen needs to be off her phone, and you continuously find her ignoring your rules, you may find yourself in an escalated power struggle if you walk over and try to take her phone away. She will want to fight back, and things can get ugly quick. Tempers flare, and the need to win escalates on both sides. I suggest that instead, you maintain your parental power without the power struggle whenever you can. For example, your teen is on her phone all night texting and losing sleep. Most phone companies now have parental controls that allow you to go online or use a phone app to shut your teen's phone off at certain hours. If your teen is not showing self-control and this becomes a concern, regulate her access to texting and the computer by setting time limits, turning the texting off, or unplugging the modem.

You can also restrict her phone to only your number when she uses the excuse that she will not be able to get a hold of you. Chances are you are paying for your teen's phone, and it is not a right, but a privilege, to own a phone. When she confronts you, you can calmly say, "I have asked you, again and again, to get off your phone, stop texting, do your homework, and go to bed. You ignore me, and every night we fight about this as you stall and stall. So as far as I'm concerned, no more phone privileges until you learn to respect my wishes."

And your teen may respond, "Well, when do I get it back?", to which you can reply, "You can start by getting your room clean, turning in your missing assignments, and being more respectful."

When you think your teen has "suffered" enough and has shown some follow through on what you have asked her to do, you can give back her privileges. The fact that you took action without a face-to-face confrontation will send the message to your teen that you will take control, that you do have the power, and that you will follow through. Teens are great manipulators and will attempt to argue, beg, plead, harass, threaten, or cry if they want something.

> **Your job as a parent is to be smarter than the situation and continue to give your teen the message that you are in charge and that you will take action (as opposed to threatening a consequence and never following through).**

Anytime you can impose a consequence without a fight or confrontation, you are more likely to have a positive outcome. This way you will stay calmer, and the situation will likely not escalate. If your teen is trashing her car and not taking good care of it, or if you find she is abusing her driving privileges (getting tickets or driving while high or intoxicated), then restrict her from the car. (In most states, if your teen takes the family car without permission, it is a felony). She can ride the school bus or get a ride from you or her friends. Even if your teen paid for her car herself, or her grandparents bought her one, you are still in charge of her driving privileges.

> **Sometimes parents get sucked into their teen's logic:**
>
> **"Dad got me that phone; you can't touch it."**
>
> **"That is my car; Grandpa gave it to me."**
>
> **"This is my room; I can do what I want with it."**
>
> **This is wrong on all accounts. As long as your teen is under eighteen and dependent on you for food and shelter, all of those things are under your rules and authority.**

One teen I was counseling told me, "My parents are so lame! I am so sick of them; I am moving in with my friend."

"And how do your parents feel about that?" I asked.

"I don't care; they can't stop me," the teen said.

"How are you going to go to school since your friend lives so far out?" I asked.

"I will drive," the teen said.

"Your parents are going to give you the car?" I asked.

"Well, they better; it's my car," the teen said.

"Didn't they buy it for you?" I asked.

"Yes, but still they gave it to me," the teen said.

"Well, yes, they did, but that doesn't mean they are going to let you take it to live with a friend they do not want you living with. The same with your phone. That is a privilege, not a right, and since they don't want you moving out, I am not so sure you are going to get all those privileges," I said.

The teen looked at me like I was crazy.

> **One of the most effective routes is to reward teens instead of withholding privileges. Describe the behavior you want to be changed in detail.**

"You have these four assignments missing in English and two in Math. If you get those in by Friday, with documentation from your teachers proving you turned them in, then you can go to the game or to your friends. Those turned-in assignments are your ticket to the weekend; if not, you stay home."

First, have the teen change the behavior, knowing exactly what the change is that you want (paint a clear picture) and then reward him or her with the privilege if he or she follows through. If not, allow no privileges. This works much better than saying, "OK, you can go out on Friday, but you have to promise me that you will clean your room on Saturday." You can bet the teen will happily promise you this and then go out, but may not clean his or her room on Saturday, or you have to do a lot of nagging to get them to do it. First, get the desired behavior; then reward.

> **Many parents give in to their teens because they do not want to feel their own painful feelings around their teen's disappointment or anger if the teen loses a privilege. And some parents give in to their teen (usually after the teen has done a great job of wearing them down with demands, tears, begging, pleading, or even throwing a fit) because they want their teen to like them. Parents fear that by setting firm limits and following through, their teen will not like them, which threatens the parents' own sense of self-worth.**

Change your strategy (be smarter than the situation, which takes your creative mind), set limits, follow through, and do not let your teen's harassing behaviors dictate your choices when it comes to discipline. Remember that your family pack will be in order if the parents are the Alphas who are in charge and leading.

If you find your teen is not respecting any of your rules by sneaking out or by being defiant, threatening, or violent, some states have "at risk" youth petitions or similarly named court orders. You can petition the juvenile court for assistance in parenting your teen. You fill out a report that describes the desired behaviors and then file it with the court. At some point, you and your teen will have a hearing. The courts can order your teen to obey curfews, have a drug and alcohol evaluation, and follow subsequent recommended treatment, family counseling, or other interventions and support. If your teen does not follow the court order and is in contempt, the judge will impose consequences, which can include a night or two in detention. Many times, teens will fear the judge and court and start complying. Many parents welcome the added external support, especially when they have tried many other consequences and the safety of their teen and themselves is at stake.

> **The bottom line is if you continue to get the same behaviors out of your teen, such as; disrespect, belittling, name calling, swearing at you, throwing fits, yelling, putting you down, storming out, coming in past curfew, punching holes in the walls, and all the other negative and aggravating behaviors teens can pull, it is because their behavior is getting *positively* reinforced. Whatever you are doing or not doing, if your teen's behavior continues, you are somehow reinforcing the unwanted behavior. You must always be smarter than the situation.**

Parenting your teen is not an easy path by any means, nor is navigating these teen years. Not everyone gets an Angel Food Cake; most bake one or more of the other specialties. You will have your own style when it comes to parenting your teen, and if you have more than one, you will most likely parent each teen differently. Keep convincing yourself that you are indeed the adult and in charge, even when your teen has worn you down. Teens need to know that their parents are in charge and that there are expectations, curfews, norms, rules, and consequences when they live under the parents' roof and authority.

Bake with confidence, and always remember that this, too, shall pass. You are at the tail end of parenting. Maybe the reason why these teen years can be so tough is to help you adjust to the sadness in your heart when your teen finally leaves the nest.

# 20

# CAKEWALK

Raising your teen will be one of the biggest challenges you face as a parent. Whether you raise an Angel or Devil's Food Cake, or anywhere in between, all of your worries, anxieties, hopes, and dreams regarding your teen will be a large part of your life.

> But, as big of a job as parenting is, it is not all of your life. There is much more to you than being a parent, and this is very important for you to remember, especially during the teen years.

Faster than you imagined, your teen will turn into a young adult and most likely leave home for college, the military, or a job. And if your teen does stay at home, he or she is no longer your legal responsibility; that part is now over. Your legal influence may be reduced to loaning your child money if he or she gets into trouble with the law or needs a co-signer for an apartment or car loan.

Other than providing your children with emotional support, financial help when needed, and advice and guidance, they are now raised; relax, breathe, and pat yourself on the back.

## YOU ARE MUCH MORE THAN A PARENT OF A TEEN

What is essential, as you are raising your teens and heading them to their adult life, is to be sure that you live your life, too. You must "fill your cup" in order to pour love and support into your family and relationships. If you do not fill your cup, you risk being stressed, irritable, overwhelmed, anxious, and depressed. For the best health for you and your family, it is imperative that you take time to do what brings you joy and makes you feel good about you!

Everyone fills his or her cup with different ingredients. Here are some you might resonate to:

- Plan coffee, lunch, or dinner dates with friends- adults only. This can be a great place to join other parents and compare notes, vent, and get support. You can even exchange recipes on raising your teen and get good ideas from other parents on how they are coping with their teens. And you can, in turn, support them with your good ideas.
- Take a class online or from your community college or adult education courses. Try some art or music lessons. Stimulate your mind in an area that stirs your passions.
- Join or start a book club. This often results in conversation and connections that begin with a book, and many book clubs become more social than book critiques.
- Go golfing, play racquetball, pickleball, or tennis, join a team sport, or go running.

- Go boating, fishing, or hiking without the kids.
- Exercise! Choose your favorite type: a walk outside, the gym, yoga, Cross Fit, Zumba, dance, or any other classes offered. Exercise is a great stress relief and provides excellent health benefits that continue long after your workout.
- Volunteer to help with an advocacy group or social services, the local hospital, your schools, or pet shelters. Find a place where your time and compassion are welcomed and appreciated.
- Plan a weekend away with your friends or your partner without your kids!
- Plan a week vacation at a resort.
- Have regular massages or spend some time at a spa.
- Have regular pedicures and manicures without taking your teen.
- Take yourself shopping without your teens, as they will want everything!

**And don't forget the little things that can help keep you sane:**

- A hot, sudsy, bubble bath, a good magazine or book, a scented candle, a glass of wine or cup of herbal tea, your favorite music, and most of all, a locked door.
- Relax in your hot tub out in the fresh air.
- Retreat to your bedroom, turn on your laptop or TV to your favorite show, and lose yourself in it.
- Cuddle up with your pet. Pets always think you are the best, and they don't demand or talk back. ("When your children are teenagers, it's important to have a dog so that someone in the house is happy to see you." Nora Ephron).
- Dance! If the teens are out and about, put on some music that gets you moving, and lose yourself in a good dance party with yourself.
- Dive into a good book or a magazine.
- Work on your Pinterest boards.

- Find a hobby: scrapbooking, painting, sculpting, photography, knitting, crocheting, making jewelry, or sitting and doing a crossword puzzle.
- Last, but not least, grab your favorite pint of Ben and Jerry's, grab a spoon, and do not share with anyone, no matter how much begging and harassment you face.

Taking care of yourself is the most important gift you can give yourself and your family during the teen years. It will distract you, relieve your stress, give you a break, and provide a mini-retreat from your frustrations and fears. Self-care will also balance your energy between being consumed by your parenting role and just taking care of you, and it will remind you that your life counts too, that you matter, and that other people enjoy you, love spending time with you, and do not want anything from you but your time and company.

This can be a far cry from your teen who can be demanding, cranky, critical of you, and generally only focused on himself or herself. Teens are self-absorbed, and parents are often sources of irritation for them.

## PUT YOURSELF FIRST AT LEAST ONCE IN A WHILE!

By putting yourself first in your life from time to time, you will fill your cup and have the emotional resources, stamina, and an attitude adjustment that will help you survive when the going gets tough and when you feel lost, frustrated, angry, and helpless.

*Is Raising Your Teen a Piece of Cake?* Certainly not always! However, even as tough as baking your Cake can be, with your tiny tot growing into your testy teen, I know you will have many delicious moments with your teen. And, when all is said and done, you can know that the main ingredient you have always added to the recipe, which makes your teen such a lucky one, is love. Keep adding this, and you can look forward to a lifelong relationship with your child. Those teen years eventually fade into the background, and the new chapters with your teen as an adult begin! Loving, worrying, and enjoying your child is a lifelong journey, encompassing many years of his or her life; those teen years from thirteen to eighteen are relatively short, considering the entire span of a lifetime.

Do the best you can, know that there are many ingredients that go into raising your teen that you cannot control, and always, always give yourself a pat on the back for all the love, energy, and care you give to your children, even when unnoticed and unappreciated as it can be during the teen years. You are the most important person in your children's lives, and they love you more than they may ever let you know.

# GLOSSARY

RAD, "Reactive Attachment Disorder," Mayo Clinic, accessed April 30th, 2019, https://www.mayoclinic.org/diseases-conditions/reactive-attachment-disorder/symptoms-causes/syc-20352939.

"Reactive Attachment Disorder," Web MD, accessed April 40th, 2019 https://www.webmd.com/mental-health/mental-health-reactive-attachment-disorder#1.

Dr. Dan Siegel: https://www.drdansiegel.com/

Dr. Dan Siegel, *Brainstorm: The Power and Purpose of the Teenage Brain* (Penguin Random House, 2013.

# ABOUT THE AUTHOR

Gail Manahan, LMHC, has been working professionally with teens and their parents for more than thirty years in her counseling practice, as a middle and high school counselor, and as the founder and facilitator of CORE (Courage/ Ownership/Respect/Empowerment) teen and adult self-growth seminars. Gail's experience gives her a wealth of information from the field on what teens want, their struggles, and just how difficult this passage of life is for them. Parents have sought Gail's help for support as they navigate through these turbulent years. Gail has been the recipient of community awards for her work with teens and is an expert and valuable resource for all who seek her professional guidance.

Gail lives in the beautiful Puget Sound area in Washington with her husband, who is a school superintendent. She has raised four teens and is now basking in the rewards of her adult kids, two of which have given her the ultimate joy: four amazing grandkids (they are all under ten years and not yet near the teen years, phew!). Gail enjoys working, writing, traveling, relaxing in the sun and reading. Her favorite parts of life are spending time with her family and friends. She approaches life with an insatiable curiosity for learning, personal growth, and loves empowering and supporting others to live their best lives.

## To Contact the Author:

Gail Manahan, LMHC, can be contacted at gail@gailmanahan.com. Join the https://www.facebook.com/GailAManahanLMHC Facebook page, or schedule private online consultations or speaking engagements with Gail. Website: Wisdom, Women, and WTF? www.gailmanahan.com.

# ACKNOWLEDGMENTS

This book is based on my experiences with teens and parents, personally and professionally. I want to thank my adult children, Erick Griswold, Jenna Buckley, Taylor Manahan, and Casey Manahan for teaching me many lessons about parenting teens. You four provided me with a variety of ingredients that not only gave me a firsthand experience of this often-difficult passage of life but gave me more empathy to support teens and parents in my professional life. You were my best teachers, and I know I could have done a better job, but I did the best I could with what I knew at the time. I wish you Angel Food Cakes when it comes to raising your Cupcakes, and I will understand and support you if you get a taste of many of the Cakes in this book. You four turned out so exceptionally well, I wonder why I was so stressed at times when I was raising you. If, as parents, we knew in advance how it would all turn out, we would sleep a lot easier!

Thank you to the thousands of teens and parents who taught me so much via my teen and adult *CORE (Courage, Ownership, Respect and Empowerment)* teen and adult seminars and my counseling practice. You taught me about every combination of every cake ingredient in this book, and that field experience taught me so much, far beyond my formal education. Being a part of all of your lives, so intimately, as you shared your truth in my office and my seminars, taught me invaluable information! The biggest lesson for me was how much you all love your family, no matter what your experience was as a teen growing up or as a parent raising your kids. I, also, listened to the guilt and pain that parents shared with me in counseling and the seminars, as parents blamed themselves for their teen's choices. I hope this book gives you some perspective and relief. Parenting is the toughest job on the planet.

Special thanks to my loving and supportive husband and co-parent, Rob Manahan, who did the best job a father can do raising our blended family. You are always my best time.

And a special thanks to my friend, Logan Taylor, for attending the teen seminars 16 years ago and leading my backup teams, co-facilitating, and being my best friend today, reading, encouraging, and helping me edit this book. You were an exceptional teen and are an exceptional adult and often my biggest fan!

Also, a special thank you to my parents, Gayle and Ruth Fixsen, for raising me, as I was a strong-willed, moody, and opinionated daughter! I apologize for all the angst I gave you and am grateful for the safe, secure, and exceptional childhood you gave me.

And, for those involved in the endless nuts and bolts of publishing, a special thank you to Jeniffer Thompson at MonkeyCMedia.com for my author's website, branding, book cover and publishing, Marni Freedman my writing coach at www.marnifreedman.com, and J. Alden for copy editing. Thank you to my beta readers for reading the manuscript and suggesting improvements from a parenting perspective. I am grateful to such an outstanding team and all of your support.

Made in the USA
Monee, IL
06 August 2022